"Larry has the heart of ⟨barcode MW01075622⟩ ... wants to
viding hope-filled enc[...]
strengthen their marria[...] in the second half of life."
Josh Mulvihill, Executive Director, Renewanation; author;
GospelShapedFamily.com

"It's a rare joy to read a book that speaks so practically and pro-
foundly to the journey of marriage in the second half of life. This
book is a gift to couples who desire not only to finish well but to
thrive together through all of life's changing seasons."
Jere Vincent, President, Family Builders Ministries, Inc.

"Grounded in the gospel and filled with practical counsel, this
book will help you not merely survive these challenges but will
also equip you to experience the sweetness of God's grace and
goodness in the midst of them."
Matthew S. Harmon, Professor of New Testament Studies,
Grace College and Grace Theological Seminary

"*A Seasoned Marriage* provides couples in the second half of their
marriage with a comprehensive handbook to help them negotiate
the latter years of married life. Every chapter contains practical
applications, and the end-of-chapter questions make this the perfect tool for a couple to study together."
Marty and Lois Machowski, Married thirty-five years;
Marty is best-selling author of *The Ology*

"*A Seasoned Marriage* contains much-needed biblical advice,
birthed in the crucible of the McCalls' own maturing marriage.
Read it. Act on it. Your life and marriage will benefit."
Terry White, Former publisher, BMH Books; retired
journalism professor

"*A Seasoned Marriage* beautifully shows how to embrace the
beauty of a relationship that matures, deepens, and flourishes
with time. It's a must-read for those seeking to grow together in
faith as the years unfold."
Mike and Becky McNamee, Founders, Legacy of Faith

"Larry guides couples navigating the unique challenges and joys of the second half of life toward a deeper, more fulfilling marriage. This book is a testament to the transformative power of God's grace in the heart of a committed relationship."

Drew and Stephanie Flamm, President and First Lady, Grace College and Grace Theological Seminary

"In *A Seasoned Marriage*, Larry offers a wealth of personal, practical, relational, and—most importantly—biblical guidance for the countless situations and experiences of later married life."

Gary Ricucci, Pastor, Sovereign Grace Church of Louisville, KY; coauthor of *Love That Lasts*

"Larry McCall has written a gem for couples in their second half of marriage. You will be blessed, equipped, and strengthened to navigate this wonderful season of marriage!"

Jim Brown, Lead Pastor, Grace Community Church, Goshen, IN; founder of Fight Club 414 men's ministry

"I'm right in the season of life that Larry is writing to and this book speaks wisdom and grace into the crucial transitions this later season of marriage is bringing my way."

Andy Farmer, Pastor; author

"As my wife and I near our third decade of marriage, we're grateful for mentors like Larry who wisely help us anticipate the years yet before us. He's a clear and wise pastoral voice for our generation!"

Marc Goodwin, Lead Pastor, Christ's Covenant Church, Winona Lake, IN

"This book is a profound manual for biblically nurturing such a grand relationship through this uncharted season of life."

Mark Chanski, Coordinator, The Reformed Baptist Network; professor of hermeneutics, Reformed Baptist Seminary; author

A SEASONED MARRIAGE

Living the Gospel
in the Middle Years and Beyond

Larry E. McCall

New
Growth
Press

newgrowthpress.com

New Growth Press, Greensboro, NC 27401
newgrowthpress.com

Cover Design: Faceout Books, faceoutstudio.com
Interior Typesetting and Ebook: Lisa Parnell, lparnellbookservices.com

ISBN: 978-1-64507-500-4 (paperback)
ISBN: 978-1-64507-502-8 (ebook)

Library of Congress Cataloging-in-Publication Data on file

Printed in the United States of America

29 28 27 26 25   1 2 3 4 5

to Gladine

You were by my side as we journeyed through our early
years of marriage, experiencing with me all the blessings
and challenges that God brought our way as we finished our
schooling, raised a family, and served our local church.
Now we are well into our second half of life and you are
still by my side as we continue to serve the Lord,
but in new ways as a "seasoned" married couple.

I thank God for you, Gladine. The proverb is true:
"He who finds a wife finds a good thing and
obtains favor from the Lord" (Proverbs 18:22).
You have been God's gracious gift to me since the day
we said, "I do" in 1975. Thank you for so faithfully and
lovingly walking the journey of life with me as together we
have sought to know Christ and make him known. I love you.

Contents

Foreword

IN THE SPRING of 1979, I stood dressed in a charcoal-gray tuxedo waiting to walk out to the front of a chapel where I, in just minutes, would see my beautiful bride coming down the center aisle to meet me. There, we would exchange rings and vows and pledge ourselves to one another till death do us part.

As I stood there pondering what was about to happen, this thought flashed through my mind:

What if she changes?

Mary Ann and I had dated for four years. It was past time for us to marry. But as I considered the vow I was about to take, I was suddenly paralyzed by the thought that this woman I loved and wanted to spend the rest of my life with might turn into someone else over time. And then what?

I remember thinking in that moment, *How does anyone do this?* How can you vow to love, honor, and cherish another person for a lifetime when you have no idea what challenges, experiences, and events will come your way that will reshape both of you?

This was the wrong moment to be having this thought! But almost as quickly as it came, another thought came to me. This one whispered to me by a still, small voice:

The only way to make a vow like this is by taking a step of faith.

I realized that my faith could not be in Mary Ann. Not because she's not trustworthy, but because she's human, just like me. And it could not be in my abilities or my strength. This step of faith I was about to take was grounded in my understanding that the same God who had called us together would guide, protect, and sustain us throughout our lifetime. And as the two of us have walked by faith—stumbling and wavering at times, but always coming back to what we know to be true about God and his love for us—we have experienced the deep joy and contentment God intends for couples to know in marriage.

I remember years later hearing an author and counselor make a bold statement that I had to pause and contemplate for a while. He said that if you don't believe Jesus and the gospel are the answer to whatever problem you're facing right now, you have not correctly understood the problem you're facing.

I remember thinking, *Is that really true?* The more I contemplated it, the more I realized that the issues we face in our life and our relationships all have gospel roots to them. Whatever the challenge, whatever the dilemma, there is a gospel root that needs to be uncovered if we hope to do more than superficially address our issue.

That's what I appreciate most about this book Larry McCall has written. I first met Larry and Gladine when I interviewed them about grandparenting. It was clear then, and it's clear again in this volume, that they understand marriage is a walk of faith and if we're going to meet the challenges we will continue to face, we must view those issues through gospel lenses. We must align our lives and our marriages with God's ultimate purposes and plans for our lives.

Both Mary Ann and I are well past the halfway point of our marriage. We've experienced the kinds of second-half issues that Larry helps us navigate in this book. As you read this, you will undoubtedly identify with the challenges he tackles. His counsel is both practical and wise. Larry understands that Jesus and the gospel provide us with the grace we need to be able to traverse the unsteady terrain that can come during the later years of marriage. He is a skilled navigator because he points us over and over again to the One who declares himself to be "the way, the truth, and the life."

Bob Lepine
Longtime cohost, *FamilyLife Today*®
Teaching Pastor, Redeemer Community Church,
Little Rock, AR

Introduction

I WONDER IF I had any idea of what I was promising. I was a starry-eyed twenty-one-year-old gazing into the mesmerizingly blue eyes of my beautiful nineteen-year-old bride. We were young. We were in love. After several years of being high school and college sweethearts, we were convinced that we were ready to get married.

On that warm first day of summer long ago, standing before two hundred of our friends and family members, I promised, "I, Larry, take you, Gladine, to be my wedded wife. To have and to hold, from this day forward, for better, for worse, for richer, for poorer, in sickness or in health, to love and to cherish till death do us part."

What Is This Book About?

Now here we are, well into the second half of our lives. By God's grace, we are still hand in hand. But life is different than it was on our wedding day decades ago. We are different. Our marriage is different. We face different issues than we did as a young married couple. And here you are, joining us on this journey of marriage in the second half of life. What are some of the more significant ways your life is different than it was when you were younger? What are some issues you are dealing with in your marriage now that you probably didn't even think about in your younger years?

In some ways, married life is easier now, isn't it? Getting by on three hours of sleep because you were up most of the night with a crying baby is a distant memory. Wondering if you can get that job that pays more so you can finally afford to buy your own house is an issue you probably don't wrestle with anymore.

But in other ways, life is harder now. The babies we stayed awake with now have lives of their own—and maybe babies of their own. How are we supposed to maintain a healthy relationship with our adult kids, some of whom have a very different worldview than we do? No longer are we struggling with getting established in life financially, but now we wonder if we have saved enough money for our latter years. Will we outlive our nest egg?

These are some of the major issues our marriages face in the second half of our lives, and there are others. How do we deal with those challenges that we didn't have to deal with in our earlier years? And—this is important—how does the gospel of God's grace shape and sweeten our marriages as we face these challenges?

Who Is This Book For?

You caught that phrase, *the second half of life*, didn't you? What's that about? Well, though our culture does everything it can to distract us from this undeniable reality, we all have an expiration date. Unless the Lord comes back during our lifetimes, we are all going to die. You don't know when and neither do I. But long ago, God's servant Moses prayed, "The years of our life are seventy, or even by reason of strength eighty; yet their span is but toil and trouble; they are soon gone, and we fly away" (Psalm 90:10). Seventy or eighty years. For some of us, our seventieth or even eightieth birthday doesn't seem all that far away. These days, many of us who live in the Western world will live to see our eightieth birthday, and some of us might even celebrate ninety years on this planet.

So what's the "second half" of life? Let's just say if you are married and you've already blown out forty or more birthday candles, this book is for you! Many of you have been married to your spouse for a long time. Your silver wedding anniversary is now a memory and your progress toward your golden wedding anniversary seems to be picking up speed. Yes, this book is for you.

Or you might be in your second half of life, but your marriage isn't all that old. Maybe you are in your second or third marriage—or maybe you just married later in life. Well, if you are married and you have crossed the likely midway point of your lifespan, this book is for you too, so stick with us.

And then there is another group of people that I hope will benefit from this book—those who care for God's people who are married and in the second half of life. Pastors and counselors who have the loving responsibility of caring for older married people can benefit from being aware of the issues seasoned couples face that younger couples most likely are not dealing with. Most marriage books and seminars seem to be for the benefit of couples either preparing for marriage or in the earlier years of their marital journey. But what about the older married couples? They are facing issues unique to this season of their lives, and many of them would benefit from wise, loving, biblical counsel from the spiritual guides in their lives. I hope you find this book helpful in your ministry.

How Can You Get the Most Out of This Book?

Some of you will read this book on your own. Maybe your spouse doesn't share your joy in reading books. That's okay. Or maybe your spouse doesn't share your faith in Christ and that's why you find yourself reading this book alone. While that adds special challenges to your marriage, God's grace is sufficient for you in your situation. I pray you find hope and help on the following pages for you as a husband or a wife.

But might your spouse join you on this journey of learning how to apply the gospel of God's grace to the issues you are facing—or will face—in your marriage? Over the years, Gladine and I have found that reading books on marriage together has led us to address issues in fresh, helpful ways that we otherwise might have missed. Going together on the journey of learning more about marriage has brought increased delight and unity in our relationship. By God's grace, you might experience the same. If your spouse doesn't enjoy reading, might you read to your spouse, or listen to an audio version together? Why not graciously invite your spouse to join you on the journey?

Yet another step you might consider is inviting close and trusted friends to join you in walking through this book. You and these other seasoned married friends could gather for a weekly or monthly discussion group, working through the book chapter by chapter.

To help you take in and put into practice what you are reading, there are questions at the end of every chapter. Some questions are for personal reflection while others are for discussion between husband and wife. If you are working through this book on your own, you can still answer the discussion questions yourself—and maybe you can look for an opportunity to share what you are learning with your spouse. If you are going through the book with friends, you can share your responses to the questions as you feel comfortable.

To truly benefit from this book, don't rush through it. Pause along the way when you encounter an issue or a Bible verse that deserves more of your attention. Meditate on it. Talk about it with your spouse. Pray over it, asking God's help as you think through how he might want you to grow in grace as you address its challenge to you. God is trustworthy. He answers prayer.

Thanks for coming with us on this journey. We are praying that the Lord will use this book in your marriage for his glory and your good.

Chapter 1

Reflecting: Why Did You Get Married in the First Place?

WHY DID YOU marry your spouse? Most of us would quickly reply, "Well, I just love him/her!" Really? What does that mean?

I've had the privilege of being a pastor for more than forty years. Over the decades, I've provided premarital counseling for more than one hundred couples. Often when I'm meeting with a couple for the first time, I'll ask, "So why do you two want to get married?" I will often ask the man first. He will say, "Well, I just love her!" And I'll respond with, "That's great! So what does that mean, that you love her?" And he'll smile awkwardly, glance at her, turn back to me and say, "You know, I just love her! She laughs at my jokes, she watches sports with me. When I'm around her, she makes me so happy! I just want to marry her and give her the opportunity to make me happy for the rest of her life!"

Okay. So I'll turn to her and ask, "And why do you want to marry this guy?" And she'll smile coyly, glance at her fiancé, reach for his hand, then look back at me and say, "Well, I just love him so much! He makes me so happy! When I'm around him, he makes me feel so special. I just want to marry him and give him the opportunity to make me happy for the rest of his life!"

Now, you know and I know that no couple actually said these words. But isn't that really the motivation behind most couples getting married? Isn't that what led you to marry your spouse—they made you happy? Isn't that why most of us got married in the first place—to give our sweetheart the opportunity to make us happy for the rest of their life?

And there is happiness—but not all the time. No spouse was ever designed to make their mate happy all the time. So what could be a better reason to get married—and *stay* married? The second half of our married years provides a wonderful opportunity for honest reflection on this foundational question and to build a better foundation for our remaining years together as husband and wife.

Even if your wedding day was long ago, let's rethink this issue now. What might be a better reason to get married? What is the purpose of marriage? Or, to ask the question a different way, "Who is marriage for?"

Marriage is not some mere social construct—the product of the culture we live in. No. Marriage is the invention of the Creator God. It was he who formed the first husband and wife. It was he who designed marriage and performed the first wedding ceremony, as it were. Genesis 2:18, 21–23 records,

> Then the LORD God said, "It is not good that the man should be alone; I will make him a helper fit for him." . . . So the LORD God caused a deep sleep to fall upon the man, and while he slept took one of his ribs and closed up its place with flesh. And the rib that the LORD God had taken from the man he made into a woman and brought her to the man. Then the man said, "This at last is bone of my bones and flesh of my flesh; she shall be called Woman, because she was taken out of Man."

Moses, the human writer of the book of Genesis, adds this important postscript: "Therefore a man shall leave his father and his mother and hold fast to his wife, and they shall become one flesh. And the man and his wife were both naked and were not ashamed" (vv. 24–25).

So if God is the Author of marriage, he has authority to delineate the purpose of marriage. And what does the sovereign Marriage Designer say was his purpose? After quoting Genesis 2:24, Paul, moved by the Holy Spirit, wrote these unexpected words in Ephesians 5:32: "This mystery is profound, and I am saying that it refers to Christ and the church."

What? Did Paul just lose his train of thought? Did he have a senior moment? Earlier in Ephesians 5, it sounds as if he is writing about marriage, but then he says that all these directives for husbands and wives refer to Christ and the church! What is that about, and how does that help us understand God's purpose in designing marriage?

Marriage Is for Christ

Have you ever thought of Jesus as a husband? Most people probably haven't. After all, Jesus was a bachelor, wasn't he? It's true that during the thirty-three years Jesus spent physically on this earth, he never married. Yet Ephesians 5:25–33 presents Jesus as a husband and his church as his bride.

Did it arouse your curiosity that Paul calls this a "mystery" in Ephesians 5:32? He says, "This mystery is profound, and I am saying it refers to Christ and the church." The word *mystery* in the New Testament does not refer to something that is unknowable, but rather to something that was not known to humans until God revealed it. *Mystery* refers to something that has been in God's sovereign playbook all along, but wasn't understood by humans until God explained it. God instituted marriage all the way back in Genesis. But what was kept hidden earlier and only revealed in the New Testament era is that he designed marriage to reflect the greatest love story ever—the love of Christ for his bride, the church.

Though our marriages bring us great happiness at times, our own happiness is not the ultimate purpose of marriage. Each of our marriages, though imperfect, has the opportunity to be a picture—a living drama—to the watching world of the loving relationship between Christ and his bride, the church. In *Loving Your Wife as Christ Loves the Church*, I wrote, "To some degree, what the world thinks of Christ and the church will come from what they see in us."[1] Sobering, isn't it?

Thinking about our calling as married couples to reflect the greatest love story ever—the love of the Perfect Husband, Jesus Christ, for his redeemed bride, the church—can make us feel inadequate, can't it? Our reflections of Christ in our marriages seem so muted, so imperfect. We all remember times as husbands and wives when we were not focused on reflecting Christ, maybe as recently as this morning. We were focused on our own frustrated attempts to get our spouse to bring us some measure of happiness—to just make us feel good about ourselves. Many of us can look back over the years humbly admitting that we sought to manipulate and pressure our spouse to make us happy. After all, that's why we married them in the first place, isn't it?

The good news is that, by God's empowering grace, we can change. Our marriages can change. We can go forward with a new perspective on the very purpose of marriage. We don't have to stay in this pattern of repeatedly trying to get our spouse to make us happy, then living with the disappointment and frustration that arise when that happiness isn't delivered in sufficient quantities. We can embrace God's ultimate purpose for our marriages to reflect Christ and his love for his bride. With the indwelling Holy Spirit's help, we can commit to "grow in the grace and knowledge of our Lord and Savior

Jesus Christ" (2 Peter 3:18). And as we are continually transformed into the image of Christ as individual Christians and as a married couple, our reflection of Christ and his love for his bride should increasingly brighten, drawing people's attention to our glorious Savior.

Marriage Is for Our Spouse

I can still recall the pain and frustration of the lowest point in our marriage. I remember asking myself, *How did we get here?* We had just had another argument. Try as I might, I could not convince Gladine that she was wrong and I was right. We were about twenty years into our marriage. There had been no adultery, no cataclysmic crisis, no call to the divorce attorney. But marriage wasn't fun anymore. Neither of us was happy.

I knew I was supposed to be loving my wife. I was familiar with Ephesians 5. In fact, I had taught that passage in various men's gatherings and even from the pulpit of our church. But I sought to justify my defensiveness and demandingness with the argument, *How am I supposed to love my wife when I don't think she's doing an adequate job of loving and respecting me? If she's not pouring adequate measures of love into my "love tank," where am I supposed to get the resources to love her back?*

I had neither the humility nor the courage to tenderly explore her heart at that moment. I was too focused on myself. But if I had, I'm sure she would have said something very similar about me. In the midst of my proud defensiveness, I had been doing a very poor job of loving her in a Christ-reflecting way. Where was she going to find the motivation to love a husband who was not loving her adequately?

We look back now, decades later, and realize that each of us had slowly slid into the selfish supposition that *marriage is for me and my spouse is supposed to be making me happy.* As in so many other stale or even deteriorating marriages, we were in this downward spiral of constantly measuring what we were "getting" from one another. Whether the issue was time together, expressions of affection, spiritual connection, or satisfying sexual intimacy, it never seemed to be enough.

Yet we knew what God was saying to us in his Word: "Husbands, love your wives, as Christ loved the church and *gave himself up for her*" (Ephesians 5:25, emphasis added). "Wives, *submit to your own husbands as to the Lord*" (Ephesians 5:22, emphasis added). Even in the realm of sexual intimacy, we knew intellectually that God's Word was clear that the focus was not "getting" but "giving." First Corinthians 7:3–4 reminds us, "The husband should give to his wife her conjugal rights, and likewise the wife to her husband. For the wife does not have authority over her own body, but the husband does. Likewise the husband does not have authority over his own body, but the wife does."

So how did the Lord graciously begin to turn our hearts away from pride and selfishness and instead toward a Christ-reflecting commitment to bring each other joy? How did God take us from living as if *marriage is for me* to *marriage is for my spouse*?

During this marital low point, we met an older Christian gentleman in our community whose wife of many years was in the latter stages of Alzheimer's disease. Each day, Bob would visit his wife in the nursing home to spoon-feed her, change her diaper, sponge-bathe her, and sing love songs to her. He did this not in one heroic act, but quietly, faithfully, day after day, week after week, month after month.

As a middle-aged, frustrated husband, I was baffled. How could this man love his wife in such tender, sacrificial ways when she was doing absolutely nothing for him? She was not fixing his meals. She was not giving him great sex. She was not speaking words of appreciation. She couldn't even remember his name. Yet day after day, he would repeat his tender, loving words and selfless, sacrificial acts. Where did Bob get the motivation to love his unresponsive wife that way? How was his "love tank" getting refilled so that he had enough to give his wife such unrequited love?

As I contemplated our older friend's amazingly joyful, sacrificial love for his wife, the Holy Spirit began to break my selfish heart. He reminded me of this simple yet profound gospel truth: "We love because he first loved us" (1 John 4:19). Bob was able to love his wife with glad sacrifice not because of what he was getting from her, but from what the Lord had already given him. He was so focused on God's immeasurable love for him that he had more than enough love to give to his Alzheimer's-stricken wife.

The Holy Spirit began to lovingly expose the selfishness and insecurity behind my defensiveness and demandingness as a husband. Simultaneously, he began to warm my cool heart with gospel hope. Loving my wife in a Christ-reflecting way went against my self-centeredness, requiring me to daily turn afresh to the Savior for his freely offered grace. And that's just where he wanted me—dependent on and fueled by his grace as I lived day by day as a husband. I had been trying to suck "life" from my wife, pressuring her to deliver if she ever expected me to reciprocate. And from my perspective, it was never enough. Like my ultimate ancestor Adam before me, I blamed my wife for my sinful attitudes and actions. My dissatisfaction discouraged her, understandably, leading us into a sad, slow, downward spiral.

The upward change in our marriage didn't happen overnight, but there was a notable reversal that we thank God for to this day. As the Spirit led me to lean into God's grace for me as a husband, I began to realize more functionally that I could love my wife—not because she was loving me (and she was, even if I wasn't admitting it), but because God loved me. I could love Gladine because "he first loved us."

Maybe as a husband, you are wrestling with some *what ifs* right now. You are aware of God's calling on you to love your wife, but *What if she just gives me the cold shoulder?*, or *What if she does nothing but disrespect me?*, or *What if she never seems to acknowledge all I've done for her?*

What if . . . ?

The truth of the gospel helps erase the *what ifs* we face. A husband's love for his wife is not dependent on her love for him, nor is a wife's love for a husband dependent on his love for her. Our love for our spouse is not a mere response to our spouse's love for us. Our love for our spouse stems from the gospel truth that Christ loves us and gave himself up for us (Ephesians 5:25). When did the Lord decide to love us? Was it when he saw us living wonderful lives as faithful followers? No. Thankfully, he did not wait for our loving faithfulness in order to love us back, or we would still be waiting for his love! Did he decide to love us when we placed our faith in him? No. It was long before that. It was before we were born, even before he created the universe. He chose to love us and adopt us as his sons and daughters even before the foundation of the world (Ephesians 1:2–6)!

Do we see what that means? God's love for us was not dependent in any way on our love for him. He decided ahead of time to love us. Now he says to us, "Husbands, love your wives, as Christ loved the church and gave himself up for her." Our love for our wives is not a response to their "lovability," but is a commitment we make independently of their worthiness or responsiveness.

Where can we husbands find the motivation—the "fuel"— to love our wives in this Christlike way? It comes from being rooted in the gospel truth that God has chosen to love us not because of our worthiness, but because of the worthiness of his Son, who stands in our place. Being fully assured of his love, I can now choose to love my wife regardless of her supposed worthiness or responsiveness. "We love because he first loved us." There were no *ifs* in our wedding vows at the beginning of our marriage, and there must not be any *ifs* in the years that follow.

Wives, resonating with the gospel truths applied to husbands, how does the gospel specifically shape and sweeten your part of the marriage? Wives are directed to "submit to your own husbands, as to the Lord" (Ephesians 5:22). That can seem so hard—even intimidating. There are so many *what ifs* that can surface in a wife's heart: *What if I think he's making the wrong decision?*, or *What if he's not the spiritual leader I think he should be?* Supporting the leadership of an imperfect husband can make a woman feel so insecure, so fearful, so . . . vulnerable.

Where is a Christian wife ever going to find the motivation to respect her husband and support his leadership in the marriage? Think of it this way: the gospel empowers a Christian woman to more clearly represent the bride of Christ, the church, as she remembers that her ministry of supporting her husband's leadership is "as to the Lord." Her decision to support her husband's leadership is not dependent on her husband's worthiness, but it's grounded on the worthiness of Jesus Christ. In fact, the preceding verse says that all members of the bride of Christ submit to one another "out of reverence for Christ" (Ephesians 5:21).

Sadly, we need to acknowledge that some wives suffer under an abusive husband. Assuming that the wife of an abusive husband is to quietly "submit" to her husband's sinful actions and words does not honor the Lord and his clearly revealed will for the marriage. A wife in an abusive marriage needs to seek safety for herself and any children living at home. She should not hesitate to seek help from her church's leaders as well as legal authorities, if needed. Her church can provide an umbrella of protection over her while dealing with her husband, calling on him to repent and counseling him toward a life that honors the Lord and reflects his love and grace.

In nonabusive relationships, gospel truths help erase those debilitating *what ifs* that a woman married to an imperfect husband understandably wrestles with. The gospel reminds a Christian wife that she is a forgiven, much-loved daughter of the High King of heaven. Because of the grace found in Jesus Christ, God the Father is smiling at her 24/7. She is safe in her loving, regal Father's hands. So even as she looks at her imperfect husband, she can look over his shoulder, as it were, and see the smile on her perfect Savior's face.

The gospel truth that God loves us not because we deserve his love but because Jesus Christ stands in our place through his perfect life and sacrificial death provides the power we need to love our spouses. And the gospel also provides the pattern of how we can love each other in our imperfect marriages:

- Because of the gospel, we love because he first loved us (1 John 4:19).
- Because of the gospel, we can accept our spouse as Christ has accepted us, not demanding certain changes to earn our acceptance (Romans 15:7).
- Because of the gospel, we can forgive our spouse's sins against us as God in Christ forgave us (Ephesians 4:32). Our forgiveness is not dependent on some sense that our spouse has sufficiently earned it.
- Because of the gospel, we have experienced the "perfect patience" of Jesus Christ (1 Timothy 1:16) and can, in turn, live with our spouse "with all humility and gentleness, with patience, bearing with one another in love" (Ephesians 4:2).
- Because of the gospel, "There is therefore now no condemnation for those who are in Christ

Jesus" (Romans 8:1). There is no need for us to
be defensive every time we detect imagined or
even real criticism from our spouse. We are safe,
not because of our own perceived goodness, but
because of the grace found in Jesus Christ.

The gospel of Jesus Christ is rich in life-giving hope and
life-changing help as we face struggles in our marriages. Rather
than feeling hopeless and helpless in seeing our spouse's failures and our own, our eyes are drawn to the limitless, unfailing love that God has for us through Jesus Christ. We are loved
by God and therefore empowered to love our spouses through
both good times and hard times. "We love because he first
loved us."

Questions

1. Looking back, how would you evaluate your reasons for
   getting married?
2. Drawing on this chapter and your own life experiences, what would you say now to a couple considering
   marriage?
3. How would a firmer grasp of the truth "We love because
   he first loved us" change the way you view your spouse
   and your marriage? Pray that God would work this truth
   deeper into your heart.
4. With your spouse, reread through the bulleted list of ways
   the gospel helps and equips us in our marriages. Then
   discuss how these truths of the gospel might work themselves out practically in your day-to-day relationship.
5. What are your hopes for your time studying this book?
   Share your hopes with your spouse and listen to theirs.

Chapter 2

Evaluating: Responding to the Changes We Are Facing

DO YOU EVER feel overwhelmed by all the changes coming into your life? Sometimes we want to say to life, *Enough! I don't need any more changes right now!* Yet if we stubbornly plant our heels and try to hold everything in its place, change keeps coming anyway and we just get run over.

Life is full of changes. Technology advances at a pace that makes our heads spin. How do our kids and grandkids keep up with all these "advances"? Cultural mores are in flux in ways that boggle our minds. Our local communities change. Stores we had shopped in for years close their doors and new ones open—stores so big we feel as if we need our GPS just to find that item we're searching for.

Many changes are not just "out there" in the world around us, but "in here"—in our families, marriages, and personal lives. Some of these are comparatively small inconveniences as we go through the second half of life, such as having to get reading glasses or realizing we are taking two pills at a time instead of two stairs at a time. Other changes are more significant, such as seeing the last of our kids move out or embracing the reality that we need to give up driving. Still other changes can be excruciating, such as walking our spouse through a life-threatening illness or facing the truth that we personally are moving toward the end of our life.

In this book, we want to openly address some of the most challenging changes married couples encounter in the second half of life. We also want to explore the crucial question of how the gospel of God's grace can shape and sweeten our response to those changes.

What Makes Change So Difficult to Accept, Let Alone Embrace?

It would be naïve to answer that question with one sweeping response. Which change are we talking about? Is it a good change or a bad change? How big—how life-impacting—might that change be? At what age are we encountering that change—fifty or eighty? And what else is going on in our lives when that change intrudes? Life can be complicated.

Yet we all have some things in common. Most of us are creatures of habit. We tend to do many of life's tasks in the same way and maybe even at the same time every day. I get up at a certain time each morning. I use the bathroom then put the coffee on. With coffee in hand, I sit in "my" chair and have my devotional time. Then it's time to do some simple exercises and take a walk in our neighborhood with Gladine. Getting cleaned up and eating breakfast come after our walk. That's the daily pattern of my morning before I head to my office. Take one of those morning routines out of the mix or even out of order and the day just doesn't feel right. And by the time we are into the second half of life, we've had many years of solidifying our habits.

But what happens if some change enters our life that, of necessity, breaks that routine? What if the doctor says I need to give up caffeine? What if having knee surgery means I can't do my daily exercises? The temptation to whine and complain about these unwelcome, uninvited changes arises in my stubborn heart. Then that Bible verse we taught our kids to memorize decades ago enters my conscience: "Do all things without grumbling or disputing" (Philippians 2:14). Yes, I am a creature of habit, but life is not constant. Life changes, and I need to change with it.

But I think there is a deeper issue that makes embracing change difficult, and that has to do with our identity. As we journey through the second half of life, we become very conscious of the aging process. In our Western culture, aging is usually associated with loss. Think of some of the losses that are associated with getting older: loss of strength and health, loss of your children living in your home, loss of the job you held in your preretirement years, loss of ministries that are now done by younger church members, loss of funds as you begin to drain your nest egg, loss of longtime friends who have preceded you to glory, loss of living independently, and eventually loss of dignity (or so it feels) as you revert to your earliest days of life in needing someone to change your diaper.

We don't like these changes. It feels as if we are losing our very identity. But are we? Is our identity truly found in the activity and productivity of our earlier years?

Maybe you were an athlete in your younger years. People knew you and praised you as a basketball player or a gymnast, but your years of athleticism are now a distant memory. Do you still try to hang on to your identity as an athlete, regularly bringing up the glory days of your physical accomplishments in your social media posts and conversations with old friends?

Or maybe you devoted a huge portion of your earlier years to being a stay-at-home mom. That's who you were— "Mom"—and you enjoyed that amazingly important role of helping raise your kids. But the house is quiet now. The kids are grown and gone. So who are you? Have you lost your identity? Are you tempted to hang on to your previous role in your now-adult kids' lives by inserting yourself into their affairs, asking detailed questions about what they're doing day after day, and offering your unsolicited advice of what they *should* be doing?

Or maybe you held a particular ministry position at your church for years. You were known as "the church treasurer" or "the kindergarten teacher." That's how your fellow church members referred to you. But the day came when a younger church member assumed "your" old ministry. Are you now critical, either privately or even publicly, of how that "new" person is doing "your" ministry? Might that reveal an unwholesome temptation to cling to your previous role as if your identity is found in what you did?

Who Are You?

Who are you really? What is your identity? Your identity is not wrapped up in what you have done in your past. It's not dependent on what you looked like or what you could accomplish when you were younger. Your identity is not found in what you've *done* but in who you *are.*

Foundationally, you are an image-bearer of God (Genesis 1:26–27). You were specially made by God to relate to him and reflect his glory. That is true no matter what you have or haven't done. That is true no matter what you can or can't do in this season of life. Your life has dignity as God's image-bearer even if the day comes when you are truly debilitated from caring for your own most basic personal hygiene.

To brighten your identity even further, as a Christian, you are an adopted child of the Most High God (Ephesians 1:3–5). You are his much-loved daughter. You are his much-loved son. He bought you with the precious blood of his Son, Jesus Christ (1 Peter 1:19). That's who you are. That's *whose* you are!

Remembering *whose* we are helps us embrace the changes we encounter in the second half of life—even changes that are difficult. We don't have to stubbornly attempt to hang on to long-held roles or reputations as if our identities or worth are wrapped up in what we accomplished in our younger years. Our identity is intact. In fact, it's immovable. We live with God-given dignity no matter what we can or can't do as our years increase. We can bask in God's love, remembering that no matter how old we are, we are his children.

Who Is He?

As our years increase, we can often respond to changes with anxiety and even fear. *My spouse seems to be more and more forgetful. What if they have the beginning stages of dementia? How far—and how fast—might that dreaded disease progress? How am I going to take care of them? What if it gets to the point that I can't take care of them? What's going to happen to me? What's going to happen to us as a married couple?* This is just one scenario that couples might face during the second half of life.

How can we counter our anxieties and fears with the reassuring gospel of Jesus Christ? We preach the gospel to ourselves in these fear-fighting, faith-building ways:

Remember the character of God. Yes, he is all-loving and yes, he is sovereign. I have reminded myself and my struggling friends to anchor our souls on these four words from our Savior: "your heavenly Father knows." Those four words are extracted from Jesus's teaching in the Sermon on the Mount as he teaches his followers to not give in to worry and anxiety. He says, "Do not be anxious, saying, 'What shall we eat?' or 'What shall we drink?' or 'What shall we wear?' For the Gentiles seek after all these things, and *your heavenly Father knows* that you need them all" (Matthew 6:31–32, emphasis added). Think about each of those four highlighted words. "Your"— our God is personal, not an abstract force. "Heavenly"—he is the Sovereign of the universe, able to meet your every need. "Father"—he loves you dearly as his son/daughter purchased

23

at the inestimable price of his Son's sacrifice. "Knows"—you and your situation are not lost in the shuffle of the world's happenings. God, your kingly Father, sees you and knows you.

Remember the saving work of God on your behalf. As we are faced with the potential for—or even the presence of—pain-delivering, loss-bringing changes, we can fight the anxiety and fear creeping into our soul by intentionally recalling what God has already done for us in the work of Christ. The biggest threats you have ever faced in life are your sin and its consequences—death and eternal condemnation. Hasn't God already graciously dealt with your biggest problems? "The sting of death is sin, and the power of sin is the law. But thanks be to God, who gives us the victory through our Lord Jesus Christ" (1 Corinthians 15:56–57). And doesn't the gospel truth of Romans 8:1 make your heart sing? "There is therefore now no condemnation for those who are in Christ Jesus." My Christian friend, if God has already dealt with your biggest problems (sin, death, condemnation) through the work of Christ on your behalf, can you not trust him to care for the lesser cares burdening your soul?

Remember the promises of God. When we are wrestling with our anxieties and fears in response to unwelcome changes looming over our lives, it is a helpful exercise to intentionally review some of the promises God has graciously given to us as his children. How reassuring to recall these words: "I am sure that neither death nor life, nor angels nor rulers, nor things present nor things to come, nor powers, nor height nor depth, nor anything else in all creation, will be able to separate us from the love of God in Christ Jesus our Lord" (Romans 8:38–39); and "My God will supply every need of yours according to his riches in glory in Christ Jesus" (Philippians 4:19). And as we age, we increasingly long for the fulfillment of the glorious promise of Revelation 21:3–4:

I heard a loud voice from the throne saying, "Behold, the dwelling place of God is with man. He will dwell with them, and they will be his people, and God himself will be with them as their God. He will wipe away every tear from their eyes, and death shall be no more, neither shall there be mourning, nor crying, nor pain anymore, for the former things have passed away."

Remember the presence of God. Why would we be anxious if we recall that our Lord is right here with us as we face the challenges of change? Our fear diminishes and our faith grows as we remember God's strong promise of Hebrews 13:5: "I will never leave you nor forsake you" (repeated from Joshua 1:5). And what was the last thing Jesus told his followers as he ascended to heaven? "Behold, I am with you always, to the end of the age" (Matthew 28:20). We are never alone. We have the promised presence of our Savior. We have his Holy Spirit indwelling us 24/7. Surely, I can cast all my anxieties on my Father's lap because he cares for me (1 Peter 5:7)!

You might counter that the unknowns still make it hard to embrace the changes God is bringing into your life in this season. It's true. God has graciously revealed some things to us, but not everything. Long ago, Moses taught the children of Israel this sobering lesson: "The secret things belong to the LORD our God, but the things that are revealed belong to us and to our children forever, that we may do all the words of this law" (Deuteronomy 29:29). You might struggle, wanting to know the *why* or the *when* or the *how long* of the trying changes you are facing, but God hasn't revealed that to you.

How do we battle our fear of all these unknowns? Let's think about this: the more we saturate our minds and hearts with what God *has* revealed, the more prepared we are to trust him with what he *has not* revealed. As a boy, I remember an older person in our church testifying, "I might not know what the future holds, but I know who holds the future." It's true, isn't it? So let us intentionally learn all we can about the character of God, the promises of God, and the work of Jesus Christ on our behalf. He is worthy of all our trust, even if we don't know what might happen to us as we journey through this latter half of life.

How Do We Help Our Spouse When Fear Is Big and Faith Is Small?

Some of you are wondering how to help your struggling spouse right now. Though you have your own struggles, you are concerned that your spouse seems to be giving way to anxiety and fear: their fear is big and their faith is small. How do we serve our spouse during these trying times of hope-draining anxiety?

First, let's not give way to the temptation to do nothing. We might not be sure what to say or do to help our spouse, so we go passive. That doesn't help. Neither does a heartless rebuke to "snap out of it!" That might drive your spouse into darker despair. Instead, seek to do the following:

Show your spouse Christ-reflecting love. Sometimes a tender hug goes a long way to express reassurance. Gently ask noncondemning questions: "What's on your heart?" "How would you like me to help you?" "How can I pray for you?" Then listen well, resisting the temptation to offer a quick fix.

Join your spouse in facing the faith-draining anxieties that are plaguing them. Offer gentle reminders of God's love and grace. "See to it, brothers and sisters, that none of you has a sinful, unbelieving heart that turns away from the living God. But encourage one another daily, as long as it is called 'Today,' so that none of you may be hardened by sin's deceitfulness" (Hebrews 3:12–13 NIV).

Pray for your spouse and with your spouse, seeking the Father's gracious help in the struggles you are facing in this difficult season of life. "Do not be anxious about anything, but in everything by prayer and supplication with thanksgiving let your requests be made known to God" (Philippians 4:6).

Stay connected to your local church. We need one another in the body of Christ as we continue our journey through this fallen world. Let's remember the teaching of Hebrews 10:23–25: "Let us hold fast the confession of our hope without wavering, for he who promised is faithful. And let us consider how to stir up one another to love and good works, not neglecting to meet together, as is the habit of some, but encouraging one another, and all the more as you see the Day drawing near."

Secondly, as we continue to face changes in the second half of life, let us anchor our souls in this glorious, reassuring truth: "Jesus Christ is the same yesterday and today and forever" (Hebrews 13:8). We are safe in his hands.

Questions

1. What kinds of changes and losses are you struggling with—or do you anticipate struggling with—the most? Check in with your spouse. Share your answers to question 1. Make a commitment to pray for each other about your struggles.

2. Where are you tempted to look for your identity? A role? An accomplishment? A talent? Possessions? Something else? According to the One who made you, what is your true identity? How can absorbing this truth help you face the inevitable changes and losses that come with age?

3. If there is something about your current situation that is not pleasing to you, is there something you can do to change it? If so, what? If not, how might God's grace help you accept it?

4. On pages 23–25 we are exhorted to remember four things. Review this list. Then choose one thing to intentionally focus on as you go through your week.

Chapter 3

Releasing: Launching Our Kids into Adult Life

NO MATTER HOW many wedding anniversaries we have celebrated, launching our kids into adult life is a benchmark for most of us. Of the major transitions many married couples face in their second half, moving from years of rearing children to the empty nest is often the first big change they have to navigate.

What are the challenges that couples face when the last of their chicks flies from the nest? What are some of the most common responses to this significant life transition, and how does the gospel shape our thinking, affections, and actions as we make this major transition, especially in the realm of our relationship as husband and wife? These are the questions we'll explore in this chapter.

The Not-So-Empty Nest

Not everyone reading this chapter can relate to the transition to the empty nest. Perhaps that's you. Do you still have at least one of your kids living with you? The phenomenon of being in your latter middle-age years or beyond and still having kids at home is becoming increasingly common in our culture. It might be that you had children later in life than some of your peers, or maybe you have a child with significant disabilities who will need your care for years to come. But for many seasoned couples, the reason they have not yet entered the empty nest years is because the "kids" they still have living in their homes aren't really kids anymore. They are of legal adult age.

The reasons for young adults remaining in their parents' home are varied. One is that many people are marrying at an older age than their parents did. Statistically, at the time of this writing, the average age for North American men to get married for the first time is 30.5 years. For women, it's 28.6.[2] Just a generation ago, when many of us were married, the average age for both men and women to marry was in their early 20s.

Though some young adult singles decide to move out of their parents' home and rent an apartment with friends or even buy their own place, many decide to remain. The economic and practical benefits of living with their parents are enticing to young adults who are furthering their education, or preparing for their upcoming wedding, or waiting for the day when they feel as if they are finally in a career they can thrive in. These young adults can enjoy the benefits of someone else paying the rent or mortgage, buying the groceries, fixing meals, and helping with the laundry.

This "extra" time with one (or more) children might be a season of delight for both the parents and the young adult child, especially if the relationship is marked by mutual respect and encouragement. The parents can enjoy additional time to be intentionally engaged in the lives of their now-adult kids, modeling a gospel-centered life and being available to give biblical counsel and life advice to their kids when asked. The younger generation can benefit from this additional time with their parents by seizing opportunities to learn "adulting" skills and, if they are believers, deepening their faith before launching on their own.

Boomerang Kids

A related experience that some seasoned couples face is having kids who had moved out at some point now returning to the nest—maybe unexpectedly. Again, the reasons for the return are mixed. Some situations are painful, eliciting our compassion: an adult child who is facing a major medical crisis or who has been abandoned by their spouse or even widowed. Or maybe they have lost their job and have been unable to find a new one. Their cash reserves are gone, and they feel they have nowhere else to turn. These young adult children of ours are in crisis mode, and we parents might be the hands and feet of Christ in showing them his compassion and mercy. Leaning on the love and grace the Lord has generously poured into us, we in turn can pour love and grace into these suffering young adults in our lives.

Some adult kids return to the nest—or maybe never left—because of other reasons, often challenging to address. Maybe there has been substance abuse, rendering the young adult child unable to keep steady employment or remain in college. Maybe the young adult is struggling with a mental illness that is so negatively life impacting that he is not safe to be living on his own. Maybe a young adult child is wrestling with such insecurities about life that launching out on her own is paralyzing. Or maybe that now-adult child seems stuck in adolescence, whiling away his day with video games and social media and binge-watching movies and TV shows rather than being a responsibly productive adult.

How is a parent of an adult child to respond when the nest isn't so empty? Whatever the reason for the child living at home, there needs to be an agreed-upon understanding of both the relationships and the responsibilities for the adult child to live with his parents for the next period of their life. If those are not clear, there will almost surely be conflict—maybe painful conflict. Here are some pointers to consider as you navigate the not-so-empty nest:

Bathe your situation in prayer. Ask the Lord to pour out his grace and wisdom as you process how to live with your young adult child. Isn't James 1:5 encouraging? "If any of you lacks wisdom, let him ask God, who gives generously to all without reproach, and it will be given him."

Talk with your spouse about your family's situation. Humbly explore one another's hearts in this time of transition. Listen carefully. Seek to come to a measure of unity on how you would like to approach the path before you.

Discuss with your child a plan for navigating the relationships and responsibilities moving forward. Eliminate as many distractions as possible—no TV in the background, no phone in hand. Maybe just a pad of paper to take notes.

- Ask your child, "What would you like to see from us as your parents?" Listen carefully and respectfully. It's likely that your son or daughter will say, "I just want to be treated as an adult. I'm not a kid anymore." Lovingly express your support of that request. That's what you want, isn't it—that your child does not stay stuck in childhood? Grant your adult child the freedom to make decisions, even if a decision leads to some sort of failure now and then. Don't give in to the temptation to always bail him out or scold him. Experience can be a great teacher, most likely accepted more readily than an unsolicited lecture from Dad or Mom.
- Discuss financial responsibilities. If your aim is to help your child move toward independence as an adult, it will be important for her to increasingly own her financial responsibilities. Will she

cover her own vehicle expenses? Help with groceries? Pay some reasonable rent? Even if you don't need her rent money to meet your own financial responsibilities, this might be a helpful arrangement for helping her be ready for launching into adulthood. You can always give it back as a surprise when she does launch.

- Discuss family schedules. While your young adult child is indeed an adult, living in a family requires respect for the schedules of other family members. Is there a designated time when your child should text if he is going to be out later than normal? Is there an expectation that he will join you for a family meal or two each week?

- Discuss household responsibilities and chores. Will your adult child be expected to care for her own laundry? Keeping her bedroom and bathroom reasonably clean? Are there certain chores that specific family members will be assigned, including your adult child? Having those spelled out can reduce the potential of misunderstanding and conflict later. "Each will have to bear his own load" (Galatians 6:5).

- Discuss family values. Without being demanding, invite your child to join you in family devotions and gatherings of your local church. Though your adult child might not share all your convictions and preferences, are there certain biblical boundaries that should be clarified and agreed upon if your adult child is going to continue living in your home? What are they? If your child cannot agree to abide by these household guidelines, then, as an adult, he is free to move out.

Notes should be taken from this parent/child meeting, reviewed and agreed upon. While this agreement doesn't need to be threatening or heavy-handed, it should be clear and respectful for all involved.

Having an adult child living in your home can be stressful not only on the parent/child relationship but also on the husband/wife relationship as well. How can you guard against unnecessary damage to your marriage in this context? A common point of contention between husbands and wives when negotiating life with adult kids at home is how much liberty and how much control the parents should have over the young adult child. Sometimes one parent will take on the responsibility for the child's difficulties by expressing, "It's all our fault. We didn't raise them right." That parent can easily become excessively permissive, enabling the young adult to remain in quasi-adolescence well into their 20s. The other parent might be disgusted with the whole scenario and attempt to become very strict and controlling. When parents are at opposite poles in relating to their adult child, it creates a wedge between them as husband and wife, and neither approach is strategically helping the adult child be ready for their belated launch (or relaunch) into adulthood.

If the not-so-empty-nest scenario is a major point of contention between the husband and wife, serious and timely action needs to be taken. The couple needs God's intervening and reconciling grace, and God gives grace to the humble (James 4:6; 1 Peter 5:5). In humility, go together to God's throne in prayer. Ask for his help and seek his direction. Might it be wise to seek advice from one of your pastors or a biblical counselor? And after a season of open discussion, prayer, and seeking counsel, you might find it necessary to ask your child to move out if their continued presence in your home continues to damage your marriage. Your marriage is "till death do us part." Your childrearing is not. Saying no to your child remaining in your home doesn't mean you don't love them. You do. And you love your spouse even more.

The Truly Empty Nest

So the day comes when the last of your kids really does fly from the nest. Maybe you've just waved goodbye as your son drove off for grad school in another state, or perhaps you've just returned from your daughter's wedding. It was a glorious day, and you're exhausted. Not just from the events of the recent weeks of preparing for the wedding and reception, but from the years of childrearing leading up to that beautiful day of witnessing your daughter and new son-in-law take the first steps into their own marriage. You've returned to your own home. Maybe one of your first thoughts after you change into some comfy clothes is, *Boy, it sure is quiet in here. Nice!* as you slip into a much-needed nap.

But then, over the next few days, reality sets in. The relief you found in your finally-quiet home begins to yield to a certain sadness. Maybe it's too quiet. You begin to sense a feeling of loss. You miss your kid's presence. You miss their activities and noise—well, at least some of it. In the coming weeks, you realize that you even begin to miss your child's friends and the friends' parents. All those conversations and noise as you drove a vehicle full of kids to games and concerts and youth group gatherings are now in the past. The conversations with your fellow parents as you sat waiting for the recital to begin or during halftime at the game are now behind you. And meal prep. Is it really worth the effort to cook a meal for just two people? And who's going to do those chores that your kids used to help with? Yeah. Maybe it's too quiet.

Then you begin to wonder, *Who am I anymore? For the last—how many years has it been? Twenty? Twenty-five? Thirty?—I've been "Mom." I used to get so tired of hearing "Mom!" for the umpteenth time each day. Now I kind of miss it. I guess I kind of liked being needed. Does anyone really need me anymore?*

It's not uncommon for a parent—often the mother—to struggle with an identity crisis in the early stages of the empty nest. Life looks very different now, maybe with the uncertainty of an uncharted road ahead and no GPS. It might be tempting to fill that void with activities that lessen the pain of loss: throwing ourselves into our jobs, hobbies, or even "ministry." But replacing the busyness of childrearing with the busyness of activities might hinder you from growth in the relationships that matter most.

So how does a married couple in the second half of life navigate their journey into the empty nest years? And how does the gospel of God's grace shape and sweeten their marriage as they continue their journey—just the two of them?

Major transitions in life—such as entering the empty nest years—provide wonderful opportunities to slow down and evaluate who you are and where God might be taking you in the years ahead. Take time to prayerfully process these relationships:

Your relationship with God. Maybe you've found too much of your identity in being a mom or a dad over the last twenty or thirty years. Now that you are no longer raising your own kids, you have an opportunity to reevaluate who you are—*whose* you are. More permanent than your role as a parent is your role as God's daughter or son. Now is the time to slow down and nurture your relationship with your heavenly Father. Invest time in getting to know your Father more intimately. Do you have a plan to seek God by reading his Word and praying on a daily basis? Why not pick a time and place where you can meet with God each day? There are plenty of Bible reading plans/apps that you can choose from. Think about what you are reading. How do you see God's character and God's grace in what you are reading? Talk to him about it. Entrust yourself to him as you pray. Entrust your spouse to him. Entrust your now-adult kids to him. You might find a new peace and joy in your soul that you have not experienced in a long time.

Your relationship with your spouse. Many couples come face-to-face with the sad—even scary—realization in the early days of the empty nest that they hardly know each other. So much time, energy, and attention was poured into the kids year after year that the husband and wife slowly drifted apart without anyone hearing the alarm bells. Now, with the kids gone, the husband and wife look across the table at one another and ask, *Who is this person?* Maybe you feel more like coworkers— "coparents"—than husband and wife.

You might find yourself at a relational crossroads. Do you go down the road of relational distance, disappointment, disillusionment, and even divorce? Some second-half couples do. The increase of marital breakups in the second half of life has even led to a new term: *gray divorce.* A growing number of older folks are seeing divorce attorneys.[3] Does it have to be that way? Might not God's grace empower you to go down the other road—the road of a gospel-sweetened marriage in your second half of life?

Even if you think, *There's no hope for our marriage—it's dead,* is not our God a miracle-working God? Isn't the One who raised Lazarus from the dead able to raise your dead marriage to life? Our all-powerful God is both able and willing to resurrect your marriage to new life. Why not humbly go to him, asking him to renew your hope in him and your love for your spouse? Talk to your spouse. Listen to each other—really listen. Pray together. Make time for each other. Read a marriage book together. Speak words of grace and love into one another's lives. Go to a marriage retreat together. Seek your pastor's or counselor's help. Growing your marriage will be a blessing to the two of you for years to come. And keeping your marriage vows through your second half of life will provide a wonderful model for those coming behind you—your kids and grandkids, as well as younger couples in your extended family and church.

Your relationship with your adult children. Though you are no longer parenting your kids in the same way as when they were younger, you are still their parent and they are still your kids. The relationship is still there, even if the roles have changed and even if you now live far apart. No longer are you in a position of authority over them. Your relationship is now more peer to peer, adult to adult. Learn to embrace and enjoy that change. It's God's way, and it should be our way too. Now, by God's grace, you can enjoy a growing, mutually encouraging relationship with your adult children for years to come. We'll look in more depth at our relationships with our adult children in the next chapter.

Launching our kids into adult life comes with such a range of emotions as parents, such a variety of blessings and challenges in our relationships with our kids and in our marriages. Through it all, we can find hope and help in God's grace as a married couple as we navigate these first rapids in a river of change.

Questions

1. If you have adult children living at home, each of you parents take some time by yourself to prayerfully consider the situation. What is going well? What is hard? What needs to change? Jot down your thoughts. Without comment or judgment, look over your spouse's list and have them look over yours. Then discuss them calmly and respectfully. In preparation for the family discussion described on pages 32–34, you might want to ask your adult child to do a similar evaluation of the situation.
2. If you and your spouse have recently become empty nesters, or if you will soon be empty nesters . . .

a. Think and pray about practical ways you can deepen relationships that have been neglected or that are now changing—with God, with your spouse, and with your adult children.

b. Discuss together how you can support each other when it's just the two of you.

Chapter 4

Transitioning: Building Relationships with Adult Children

ONCE A PARENT, always a parent. But it's different now that our kids are no longer under our daily care and authority, isn't it? Now they are adults living their own lives. Where are we supposed to learn how to build enjoyable, loving relationships with our adult kids and kids-in-law? Isn't it fascinating that while there are scads of books, sermons, podcasts, and seminars available on parenting, nearly all of them are geared for the parents who are currently raising their kids? Yet with longer life spans these days, many people have more years parenting adult kids than they had parenting children at home.

Navigating the journey of being parents of adults is uncharted waters for most of us. We love our kids, yet understanding our role in their lives seems unclear. We want to have a good relationship with them—one marked by joy—but often the relationship feels tentative, even strained. Are we too involved in their lives? Not involved enough? How much of our involvement do they want? How do we sort our relationships as adults of different generations in the same family?

More importantly, what is God's calling on us as the older generation? And how does the gospel of God's grace inform and empower us to build life-giving relationships with our adult children and their spouses, healing past wounds and building adult-to-adult relationships that are a blessing to all?

The Desires of Our Hearts

What was on your heart as you were raising your children? What was your hope for them? How did you pray for them? If you were already a follower of Jesus during your childrearing years, wasn't the passion of your heart to raise your kids so that they would, in God's kindness, follow in your steps to love God and serve him in the family, the church, the community, and the world? You wanted to be able to echo the words of the apostle John: "I have no greater joy than to hear that my children are walking in the truth" (3 John v. 4). For some parents, that has been a grace-saturated reality. And for others, that has not been the case—at least not at this time.

The Challenges We Face as Parents of Adult Children

There can be many delights in being parents of adult children: being friends, enjoying life experiences together, and offering practical help and words of encouragement as we go through life. But there are often challenges too. What are some of the common issues that many seasoned couples encounter in being parents to adult children?

Geographical Distance. One often-experienced family obstacle many seasoned couples face is that of distance. Maybe you dreamed that your kids would marry a local sweetheart and settle into a home near yours, giving you lots of opportunities to interact with them and your future grandchildren. But that didn't happen. Your child, whether married or single, lives far away. How does the gospel of God's grace help a parent work through the challenge of living a long distance from their adult kids?

There is a cost involved in pursuing a relationship with kids who live far away, isn't there? We sacrifice time to be with them—time away from our home, our work, and our regular responsibilities. We invest our money to make trips to see them. Yes, it can be a sacrifice, especially for parents with busy schedules and limited financial resources. But didn't our Lord sacrifice to come to us? Recalling his immeasurable grace to us empowers us to loosen our grip on our calendars and finances so that we can give of ourselves in seeking a growing, healthy relationship with our adult kids who live far away. And thankfully, in our technologically advanced era, we can have virtual proximity through texts, phone calls, and video chats. Distance from our adult kids might be a hurdle to jump, but it doesn't have to be an insurmountable obstacle to a close relationship.

Crises. Some challenges are more volatile than those of distance. Some difficulties that parents of adult children face deserve the word *crisis.* Sometimes our kids experience crises so severe, they keep us awake at night and, Lord willing, keep us on our knees. Maybe your adult child or child-in-law is undergoing a major medical or mental health crisis. Your heart aches for them, but you can't fix it. You can't make it go away. But by God's grace, you might be able to help. Sometimes having Mom or Dad—or even better, Mom *and* Dad—present provides comfort to an adult child who is walking through such a crisis. Asking "How can we help?" reflects the grace of Christ to our hurting family members.

Maybe the crisis your adult child is going through is not health related, but financial. Other adult children might be struggling with substance abuse or some other addiction. How can parents help in these situations? On one hand, it would not be reflecting the love of Christ to just look away with a *that's their problem* attitude, but neither would it be beneficial to enable the adult child by trying to protect them from the natural consequences of their own poor decisions in life.

Sometimes seasoned couples find themselves at odds with one another in how to respond to their hurting kids. One is bent toward rescuing their troubled child, and the other is taking a "tough love" stance. As much as we love our adult children, we cannot let their current crisis destroy our marriage bonds. Seek the Lord's wisdom together. Ask him to unite you on how to approach your in-crisis child. Talk to one another graciously. Listen to one another humbly. Get counsel from trusted spiritual advisors, if needed. Then, once there is an agreed-upon approach to your child's crisis, move forward together as a united agent of God's help.

Divorce. This is a heartbreaking experience that many families go through. Not only is there a separation between the previously married husband and wife, but divorce can also bring painful collateral damage as other family relationships are torn apart. In addition to grieving over the trauma your own child is experiencing with the breakup of their marriage, maybe you are mourning your relationship with your child-in-law, which is now strained or has been lost altogether. And what about the grandkids? Your heart is breaking for them too.

In *Grandparenting with Grace*, I wrote this counsel in guarding your heart against despair as the parents of a child experiencing the trauma of divorce:

> First, let me encourage you to open your own hurting heart to your heavenly Father. What truth does 1 Peter 5:6–8 remind us of? "Humble yourselves, therefore, under the mighty hand of God so that at the proper time he may exalt you, casting all your anxieties on him, because he cares for you." If your heart is aching right now with the pain and complications that have been inflicted on your family due to the divorce of one of your kids, may I ask you to pause in your reading and reflect on that astonishing phrase at the end of 1 Peter 5:8? "He cares for you." Think about that. The sovereign King of the universe is also

your heavenly Father. He has already demonstrated his mind-blowing, heart-melting, eternity-changing love for you in sending his precious Son to die in your place (Romans 5:8). Now, view your current family relationships looking through the lens of that gospel truth. Though your family is going through painful times, you are not outside of your heavenly Father's love. His love for you has already been demonstrated in the manger of Bethlehem and the cross of Calvary. He cares for you as his beloved child. With your heart anchored in that love, "cast all your anxieties on him." Go into your heavenly Father's throne room laying your pain and confusion on his divine lap knowing that he is both willing and able to care for your situation.[4]

It would not be surprising for a parent to feel bitterness toward the one they see as the guilty party in bringing this pain of divorce upon the family. Sometimes the parents realize it was their own child who prompted the divorce, bringing pain and possibly even stirring anger over their child's actions. In other situations, "the guilty party" is assumed to be their child's ex-spouse, with the parents considering their own child as "the victim."

The reality, though, is that nearly every marriage struggle has *two* guilty parties, not one. It might be true that one spouse was the primary instigator of the divorce, but attributing all the blame to their child or their child-in-law is probably a misrepresentation of the situation. Playing the blame game might do more harm than good. Going down the path of bitterness and blame might inhibit opportunities to point the hurting family members to God's grace. Those of us in the older generation can be gentle models of grace-fueled love and forgiveness. This might feel impossible when we feel overcome with grief and even anger. But we can help each other as husbands and wives in reminding each other of the grace we've experienced from our Savior. Then, with tears on our cheeks and aches in our hearts, we can reflect that grace to our family, lovingly praying for repentance and reconciliation for all involved in this painful division. We can choose to forgive the one(s) bringing this trauma to our family not because they *deserve* our forgiveness, but because "God in Christ forgave you" (Ephesians 4:32). We can love them not because they *deserve* our love, but because Christ first loved us (1 John 4:19).

As the older generation, we seasoned couples can serve as anchors in these tumultuous situations to the grandchildren whose lives are being rocked in the storm of their parents' divorce. Our grandchildren might need us more than ever in these trying times. We can reflect our Savior's love and grace as we carefully and compassionately listen to their hearts. We can speak gently, acknowledging their pain, expressing our love for them, and reminding them of the greatest, most unshakeable love of all—God's love for them.

Rejection. One of the confusing and even painful issues that seasoned couples sometimes face with their adult children is that of rejection. By that I mean adult children who have rejected the views and values their parents sought to impart to them during their growing-up years. The rejection of the parents' perspectives might have come in one painful announcement, or it might be more the result of a gradual drift away from the parents' convictions and teaching, bringing an awkwardness to the relationship. Some adult children will walk away from the political and social views of their parents, adopting popular positions among their generational peers. While these political and social divergences might not be as heartbreaking as some other issues we've looked at, they can be confusing, making the intergenerational relationship awkward and tentative, with the parents feeling as if they are walking on eggshells in family conversations.

Sometimes an adult child will abandon the morals he was raised with in a Christian home, embracing and promoting positions and practices on sexual issues that break the parents' hearts, such as promiscuity, cohabiting with someone of the opposite sex, pursuing transgender lifestyles or gay relationships, maybe even including same-sex "marriage."

Especially grievous to parents is the plight of their children who choose to abandon their parents' faith in Jesus Christ and commitment to his Word, the Bible. How should parents maintain a God-honoring, loving relationship with adult children who have rejected the parents' personal faith and years-long teaching that salvation is found in Christ alone by grace alone? Consider these applications of the gospel in your relationships with your adult children.

Deal with Past Wounds in the Safety of the Gospel

Some parents, having especially sensitive consciences, assume blame for the adult child's decision to depart from the beliefs and life commitments of the older generation: *it's all my fault*. Well, probably not. The gospel reminds us that we are all sinners: "For all have sinned and fall short of the glory of God" (Romans 3:23). That includes our adult children. Every human being on this fallen planet has been born as an image-bearer of God. Our status as image-bearers includes the ability to make choices. Except for Jesus Christ, every human being sometimes makes sinful choices. And the Bible is clear that "each of us will give an account of himself to God" (Romans 14:12).

Other parents dismiss any role they might have had in their adult child's departure from what they were taught growing up: *it's not my fault*. While we don't necessarily know what's in the heart of a parent who takes this posture toward their "wayward" child, that reaction of dismissing any blame might be the ugly fruit of pride. Maybe this parent is so frustrated with his adult child that he slams the relational door and locks it, breaking contact with his son or daughter.

Thankfully, the gospel of Jesus Christ offers us a better way than either extreme. It can be applied in very practical ways to our hearts and relationships when we find our adult children going in a very different direction from what we ever dreamed or desired. The gospel reminds us that we are all sinners. Admitting that reality should produce a measure of humility in our lives. While we don't assume all the blame for the sin of our children, neither do we dismiss any sin we might have contributed to the division we are experiencing in our relationship with them. The gospel also reminds us that God's grace is available to us, not because we are good people but because Jesus was good on our behalf. He lived the life we should have lived, but didn't. Then Jesus died the death we should have died for our rebellion, but didn't.

Remembering that gospel truth brings hope. Shaped by both gospel humility and gospel hope, we can explore our lives, praying sincerely, "Search me, O God, and know my heart! Try me and know my thoughts! And see if there be any grievous way in me, and lead me in the way everlasting!" (Psalm 139:23–24). As the Holy Spirit reveals our sin to us—whether recent sin or sin from our years of childrearing—we can confess that to the Lord, receiving his forgiveness. Then, knowing our security with God because of the forgiveness we have in Christ, we can humbly and freely confess any sin against our child that the Lord has surfaced in our consciences, asking for their forgiveness.

This confession and request for forgiveness must be free and full. No excuses given to minimize our sin. No demands for the child to reciprocate with their own confession of sin toward us. If our adult child grants us forgiveness, our response is that of genuine thanks, seeking to live a life of humble authenticity before them, showing them the life-transforming effects of the gospel in our own lives. Confessing our sin can bring healing (James 5:16).

Of course, if the Spirit moves our child to respond with their own confession of sin and request for forgiveness, we must forgive even as we have been forgiven (Colossians 3:13).

Face the Present Challenges in the Power of the Gospel

If we parents feel hurt by the choices our children have made to depart from our beliefs and morals, we can wrongly respond by trying to make them come to their senses, attempting to change them through our own efforts. Maybe we try to shame them through our lectures; manipulative, passive-aggressive remarks; or even our nonverbal reactions to their viewpoints and lifestyles. But when we try to play the role of the Holy Spirit in our kids' lives, we often do more harm than good. If trust between us and our adult children is strained to the breaking point (or is already broken), how might that trust be restored? How might the fruit of the gospel in our lives as parents be a tool used by the Holy Spirit to heal some of the rift between the generations?

Isn't it interesting that both James and Peter quote Proverbs 3:34 that God opposes the proud but gives grace to the humble (James 4:6; 1 Peter 5:5)? If the Holy Spirit repeatedly draws attention to the connection between our humility and God's grace, we should be sitting up and taking notice! We need God's grace in healing our broken relationships, and God gives grace to the humble.

Gospel-empowered humility moves us away from our bent to proudly proclaim our views to our kids, and instead helps us humbly listen to their hearts (whether we agree or not). "Let every person be quick to hear, slow to speak, slow to anger" (James 1:19). So to build trust with our adult children who have chosen a path in life different from ours, we seek to understand before seeking to be understood. We can genuinely ask open questions such as, *Would you help me understand why you see that issue that way?* Then respond with truly listening rather than quickly retorting with your own view. Showing respect by seeking to understand their world and their viewpoints can be a tool in rebuilding bridges. Maybe someday they will reciprocate by asking the reasons for our beliefs, but until then, we thank them for sharing their views and affirm our love and respect for them as adults, even if we don't see eye to eye on certain issues.

And we pray. We pray for our own hearts to be humble and loving, bearing with relational pain without becoming hardened or resentful or cynical. We pray for our spouse and our marriage that we might share this parental concern together, seeking God's help in being unified while we navigate the rough waters our family is going through. We pray for God's work in the lives of our children, asking the Spirit to shine "the light of the knowledge of the glory of God in the face of Jesus Christ" into their hearts (2 Corinthians 4:6).

Look to the Future with the Hope of the Gospel

With our hope firmly anchored in the trustworthy character of our gracious, sovereign God, we continue to move forward with gospel-fueled faith that he changes lives. Though our adult children might continue to chart a course in life that diverges greatly from our own path and preference, we can continue to love them as we have first been loved by our heavenly Father. Even if our kids are far from God and us, we can reflect the prodigal son's Father in Luke 15:11–32 (a picture of God himself) by standing at the door of our family, as it were, with the door open for our kids to come home to our glad embrace.

Grow in Your Marriage Through It All

As a married couple making this challenging journey of parenting adult kids, remember the priority God has given to your marriage. As much as you want to enjoy your adult children through the good times and help them through the hard times, don't allow your devotion to your kids to have a destructive effect on your marriage. Invest in your marriage. Intentionally remind your spouse on a regular basis of the love that God has for you both and the power of his grace in your daily life together. Pray *for* one another. Pray *with* one another, and in God's grace, your union will provide for the coming generations a powerful example of a marriage shaped and sweetened by his gospel.

Questions

1. Think back to the desires you had for your children as you were raising them. Are you currently experiencing disappointment that some of those desires have not—at least so far—been fulfilled? Now evaluate your desires. Are there some you need to let go of—desires that were perhaps not godly? Are there unfulfilled godly desires that you need to place in God's hands and leave there?

2. Do you tend to blame yourself for your adult children's problems and beliefs? Or do you tend to blame them and absolve yourself? Reread pages 47–49 then pray, asking God to search your heart and give you an accurate view of yourself and your children.

3. How have you tried to be the Holy Spirit in your children's lives, or when do you find yourself tempted to try? Do you have a hard time just listening to their beliefs and opinions in order to understand? Do you find yourself interrupting, lecturing, cajoling, manipulating, rolling your eyes, or being passive-aggressive? Pray for humility

and hope in your relationships with your children. Consider asking your spouse to give you a gentle signal when they see that you are beginning to give in to your unhelpful impulses.

4. Discuss with your spouse how you think you are doing as a team as you navigate difficulties in your relationships with your children. Talk about whether there are things you could be doing better together. And pray.

Chapter 5

Resisting: Fighting the Tendency Toward Marital Monotony

AFTER YEARS OF marriage, we found ourselves no longer in marital bliss, but marital monotony. Our marriage wasn't fun anymore. Neither of us had threatened divorce, but if you were to compare our marriage to a hot air balloon, we had clearly lost heat. The gondola of our relationship was barely airborne, bumping along the rough terrain of life.

Sadly, the story of our monotonous midlife marriage is all too common. Many married couples gradually drift apart over the years until something or Someone awakens one spouse or the other to the sad reality of the distance between them. Even if they are still legally married to one another, they might feel more like roommates or coworkers than husband and wife. The memories of the joy and intimacy they experienced in the early days of marriage now seem like someone else's story—not their own. How did their marriage lose its luster? Can they ever regain their lost "heat" and thrive in their marriage as they travel the second half of life?

How Did We Drift So Far Apart?

Many couples arrive at the second half of their lives having given little attention to their marriages for years, often because children have been taking up most of their time and energy.

It's possible that the early days of their marriage were marked by deep delight in one another. Then life happened. Perhaps children came along, and they required so much time and energy that focusing on one another as husband and wife took a back seat. And there were growing careers and the demands of home ownership. Finding time—making time—to nurture the marriage just didn't seem that realistic with everything else needing attention.

So the drift began, maybe slowly at first, but eventually the previous closeness they had felt in their early days now seemed like a distant memory. Now, in the second half of life, the kids are grown, no longer needing the constant attention from Mom and Dad. It's just the two of them again, and it feels as if it's time for a DTR talk. It's time to "define the relationship."

Let's say it's the wife who first feels the distance between her and her husband. Maybe she brings it up to him but is disappointed when he doesn't seem to have the same level of concern. In her disappointment, she takes another step away, hoping to find a measure of happiness elsewhere, spending more time with friends, family members, or even hoping for virtual connections as she scrolls through social media. Then maybe the husband feels her lack of admiration and approval, so he takes his own step away, seeking affirmation at work, in sports, or even the false intimacy of porn. On it goes, with each spouse reacting to the other's step away by adding their own. And the relational gap grows.

Over time, the untended marriage has become noticeably distant and disappointing to both husband and wife. The last safety net they have to keep them from crashing into the wall of divorce is their Christian commitment to stay married "till death do us part." So they settle into staying married legally, even if it feels as if they are relationally divorced. To minimize conflict and to avoid at least some of the pain of their disappointing marriage, they keep their distance, interacting with one another out of duty more than delight.

But is that what any married couple really wants? Is that what God really wants for a couple as they journey through the second half of their lives?

What Does God Want Our Marriages to Be Like?

In chapter 1, we explored the profound implication of Ephesians 5:32 that God designed our marriages to be living reenactments of the greatest love story ever: the love that Christ has for his bride, the church. In that verse, Paul clarified why our marriages are so important: "This mystery is profound, and I am saying that it refers to Christ and the church." Christ is the Husband to his wife, the church, and God wants us as married couples to shine the glory of Christ into our dark world by reflecting his amazing love for his bride. That's the gospel purpose for our marriages.

Embracing God's high calling on our marriage should awaken us to the reality that we were never meant to live with such distance from our spouses. As the Spirit convicts us that living this way is not what God wants, we are stirred to ask, *How can we change? How can our marriage be marked with joy again? How can we have a Christ-reflecting, thriving marriage in the second half of life?*

Where Can We Find Hope and Help for Our Marriages in the Second Half of Life?

Marital renewal is more than a self-help project. We're not going to find the motivation or the strength we need to transform our marriages by looking in the mirror, giving ourselves some sort of pep talk. The power to transform our marriages doesn't lie within our spouse either. If we think that we can somehow guilt or pressure our spouse to bring about the changes we desire, we are going to frustrate our spouse and disappoint ourselves.

If our marriages are going to thrive in this season of life, we need to look higher and further than ourselves. We need to look up. We need God's help. Are you ready for some good news? The Bible says, "His divine power has granted to us all things that pertain to life and godliness, through the knowledge of him who called us to his own glory and excellence" (2 Peter 1:3).

Have you ever found yourself thinking—or even muttering under your breath, *They will never change*? Maybe any hope you had for experiencing a loving closeness to your spouse evaporated a long time ago. *Oh*, you think, *being close to a spouse in the second half of life might work for some couples, but not me.* Your situation is different. You've tried to get your spouse to change, but nothing worked. Your marriage is stuck. Your marriage is hopeless.

Listen, my Christian friend, your marriage is far from hopeless! Think about this: if Jesus could raise a dead body to life, isn't he able to raise a dead marriage to life? Do you remember the interaction between Jesus and Martha right before Jesus raised Martha's brother, Lazarus, from the dead? "Jesus says to her, 'I am the resurrection and the life. Whoever believes in me, though he die, yet shall he live, and everyone who lives and believes in me shall never die. Do you believe this?'" (John 11:25–26). That question, "Do you believe this?" grabs our attention, doesn't it? So, do you? Do you believe that Jesus can raise your marriage back to life? That he can breathe fresh life into you and your spouse, transforming your marriage into a relationship that brings him glory and brings you joy?

How does the Lord do that for us? Has he given us a list of rules and sternly admonished us, *Just do it! Try harder!*? The "just try harder" method never seems to last too long, does it? We fail, try again, fail again, then just give up. There has got to be a better way.

There *is* a better way. In the New Testament book of Titus, Paul explains how ordinary Christians can live noticeably different than they did in their before-Christ days—different from their relatives and neighbors who haven't put their trust in Jesus. He explains in hope-fueling ways how God has given us a "trainer" so that we ordinary Christians can live Christ-reflecting, transformed lives. What trainer has God given us? "For the grace of God has appeared, bringing salvation for all people, training us to renounce ungodliness and worldly passions, and to live self-controlled, upright, and godly lives in the present age" (Titus 2:11–12).

Our trainer is "the grace of God"! Yes, there are commands in Bible, including commands that directly relate to our marriages, such as "Wives, submit to your own husbands" (Ephesians 5:22) and "Husbands, love your wives" (v. 25). But the motivation and power to obey these commands is not found in ourselves. We find our ability to obey God's directives, including those that directly affect our marriages, not in ourselves, but in the grace of God—the gospel of Jesus Christ applied by the Holy Spirit working in our lives.

What Does the Gospel Bring That Shapes and Sweetens Our Marriages in the Second Half?

The gospel brings clarity. The gospel reminds us that the struggles we face in our marriages are more than differences in personalities or family backgrounds. Underlying the various challenges we face in feeling "one" with our spouse is a spiritual battle. Satan hates Christ, and because our marriages are designed to reflect Christ and his love for his bride, our adversary wants to do what he can to demean the reputation of our

Lord by attacking our husband/wife relationship. The enemy is not our spouse. The enemy is Satan.

The gospel brings faith. The gospel displaces our sinful cynicism that *nothing will ever change* with a growing faith that God can revive our marriage for his glory and our good. "And I am sure of this, that he who began a good work in you will bring it to completion at the day of Jesus Christ" (Philippians 1:6).

The gospel brings humility. The gospel leads me to see my own sinful contributions to our marriage struggles. Acknowledging my own sin shapes my approach to problems in our marriage, leading me to examine my own heart in the midst of the problems we are facing. "What causes quarrels and what causes fights among you? Is it not this, that your passions are at war *within* you?" (James 4:1, emphasis added). Admitting that my own sin is my responsibility in marriage conflict will lead me to evaluate and seek to extricate the "log" from my own eye before attempting surgery on the speck in my spouse's eye (Matthew 7:3–5).

The gospel brings repentance. The gospel reminds me of the riches of God's kindness and forbearance and patience toward me, leading me to repentance (Romans 2:4). Recalling his grace to me compels me to stop my movement away from him and my spouse, turning me around so I can now move toward God and my spouse.

The gospel brings forgiveness. In the gospel, I learn that "we have redemption through his blood, the forgiveness of our trespasses, according to the riches of his grace" (Ephesians 1:7). The pattern of a gospel-centered marriage is one in which a forgiven husband and a forgiven wife are "kind to one another, tenderhearted, forgiving one another, as God in Christ forgave you" (Ephesians 4:32). Forgiven sinners forgive sinners.

The gospel brings acceptance. The gospel reminds me that I must not require my spouse to change in certain ways before I will accept them. Rather than placing conditions on my spouse before I will receive them into my life, I am to welcome my spouse even as Christ has welcomed me to share his life for the glory of God (Romans 15:7).

The gospel brings love. "The greatest of these is love" (1 Corinthians 13:13). Here is the capstone of all the gifts that come to us because of the gospel. How does this transform our marriages? Our tendency is to love our spouses when they seem most "loveable" to us. But if your marriage has been distant at best and painful at worst, it might be hard to find enough "lovability" in your spouse to love them back. The gospel reminds us that "we love because he first loved us" (1 John 4:19). Our love for our spouse is not dependent on our spouse. It relies on the love we have already received from God because of Jesus Christ and his work on our behalf.

What Steps Can We Take to Move Closer Together in This Season of Life?

As the grace of God continues its work of stirring fresh hope in our hearts, progressively transforming us to be greater reflectors of Christ, what practical steps might we take to move toward our spouses rather than away from them?

Confess your sin to your spouse and ask forgiveness. It's usually our pride that keeps us from acknowledging our sins against our spouse. But there is safety in the gospel. We are no longer under condemnation (Romans 8:1–4), so there is no need for defending ourselves by denying or minimizing our sin. We can come to our spouse, knowing that the Lord has forgiven us and now humbly asking our spouse to do the same so our marriages might be healed (James 5:16).

Forgive your spouse's sin against you. Though there are no strings attached to our own confession and request for forgiveness, if our spouse approaches us confessing their sin and requesting our forgiveness, we can forgive fully and freely. Colossians 3:13 directs us: "As the Lord has forgiven you, so you also must forgive." Holding on to a long-held grudge from sins that are now being brought into the light and refusing to give the gift of forgiveness is not only sin, but it also bars the way to marital closeness. Forgiveness, on the other hand, opens the door to reconciliation with your spouse. If the sin that is being confessed by your spouse has caused especially deep damage to your soul and your relationship, such as adultery or abuse, seeking outside help might be not only helpful but also necessary in understanding how to begin the long journey to forgiveness and reconciliation.

Make time to hear your spouse's heart. Especially if you've been distant from your spouse for some time, you might be out of touch with what they are truly feeling. How might you draw out what is deeply embedded in their heart (Proverbs 20:5)? Make time to talk together. Express your heartfelt love for your spouse and your desire to truly listen, longing to understand their heart. Asking open questions about things that really matter can be so helpful in drawing the two of you closer together. If you're not sure where to start, you can always ask questions such as "What's on your heart?" or "How can I better encourage you?" or "How would you like me to be praying for you in this part of our journey together?" Their answers can lead to further heart-exploring questions.

Listen well. If your marriage has been marked by discord and distance, it's quite probable that you haven't been truly listening to one another. Often when a couple is in conflict, one spouse is not really listening when the other is speaking. Maybe they've developed the habit of tuning out their spouse, assuming *I've heard it all before* as they form their retort even before their spouse finishes their sentence. But the grace of God can make us more loving and patient with one another.

So we listen humbly, and we listen carefully. We make eye contact and communicate with nonverbal methods—humbly nodding our acknowledgment of what has been said or tenderly taking their hand—that we really do care. We gently ask questions of clarification if needed, reflecting back what we've heard and verbally expressing affirmation.

Spend daily time together. If you want to close the gap between you and your spouse, intentionally do more daily activities together. Maybe you could work together in the kitchen, run errands together, take walks, eat meals together (with no screens to distract you!), and go to bed at the same time most evenings. Sharing daily life can be bonding. It's worth the effort.

Learn together. When was the last time you read God's Word together or prayed together? Spending time pursuing God as a couple can do wonders in healing relationships that have drifted apart. Over the years, Gladine and I have enjoyed reading Christian books on marriage together and going to marriage seminars when we can. Listening to Christian audiobooks or podcasts might be more your cup of tea as a couple. Look for ways to grow in Christ together.

Honor one another. There is one area of competitiveness between a husband and wife that can actually be helpful in closing a relational gap in their marriage: "Outdo one another in showing honor" (Romans 12:10). Isn't it interesting that both husbands and wives are explicitly told in God's Word to show honor to one another? Wives are directed in Ephesians 5:33, "Let the wife see that she respects her husband," and in 1 Peter 3:7, husbands are told to show their wives "honor." We do that in how we speak *to* one another when we show gratitude and affirmation. We honor our spouses, too, in how we speak *of* them to others. Proverbs 31:12 says of the ideal wife, "She does him good, and not harm, all the days of her life." And the husband honors his wife as he praises her: "Many women have done excellently, but you surpass them all" (v. 29). Our actions can show honor to our spouse as well. Isn't it encouraging to see a man treating his wife with honor as he opens the door for her or assists her with putting on her jacket, or a wife who takes her husband's arm in a way that says, *I'm with him!?*

Delight in one another. Remember those earlier days of your marriage that exuded joy? You could hardly wait to be together after being apart. There were smiles and hugs and kisses and laughter and love-making. Here's an idea: read aloud the Song of Solomon together with the husband reading his parts and the wife hers. That exercise might help rekindle the fire! We don't need to outgrow delight in our marriages. Instead, that joy in one another can continue to grow even as we journey into our older years hand in hand.

Say "I love you" throughout the day. It's hard to beat saying and hearing those three precious words. When might you make a point of giving your spouse those tender, reassuring words? When you wake up? When you leave for the day? When you come home? When you are ready to go to sleep? When you appreciate something special your spouse has just done? Or for no particular reason at all! If you've fallen out of the habit of being verbal with your love, today would be a great day to resurrect that wonderful habit. May any monotony you've felt in recent years give way to joy.

What Are the Benefits of Having a Joyful Marriage in the Second Half?

Going through the second half of life with a spouse we find delight in obviously makes our own lives more enjoyable. We find ourselves regularly thanking God for the blessing of a spouse who loves us and thanking God for the privilege of serving this wonderful person we're married to. *We* benefit from pursuing a close, happy marriage.

Those coming behind us benefit as well. Our own kids and grandkids are blessed to see the example of the effectiveness of the gospel in our lives and in our union as husband and wife. This legacy of our long and loving marriage can encourage hope in the hearts of those couples younger than us as they go through the blessings and challenges of their own marriages. Seeing God's grace in helping our marriage not only survive but also thrive encourages them to seek God's gracious help, as well, for their own marriage to prosper.

Christ is honored as we reflect him and his love for his bride not only in the emotionally charged early years of matrimony but also in the seasoned years as a married couple finishing our journey together with joy in him and in one another.

Questions

1. How close would you say you are to your spouse compared to when you were newly married?

2. If you feel you've drifted apart, what factors would you say created distance between you? If you feel as close as you were—or even closer—what do you think enabled you to maintain or even increase that closeness?

3. Which benefits of the gospel—clarity, faith, humility, repentance, forgiveness, acceptance, love (pp. 57–59)—do you think are most needed right now to begin improving your marriage? Pray that God would work these benefits in your hearts so that they would bear fruit in your relationship.

4. What might be an issue that your spouse has wanted to talk about, but that you have avoided? What needs to happen for you to engage in that conversation?

5. Review the practical steps for moving closer together (pp. 59–62). Choose one or two of these steps to focus on in the coming weeks. Pray that God would enable you to put

them into practice. Set up reminders for yourself. And if possible, enlist a close friend to pray for you and hold you accountable.

Chapter 6

Helping: The Challenges of Aging Parents

HAVE YOU EVER noticed that God's commandment to "honor your father and your mother" (Exodus 20:12) has no age limit? That's not a commandment God threw in just for kids. It's for people of all ages. Honoring our parents is a calling from God as long as they live. But as our parents slide into their elderly years, how does God want us to help them with the growing concerns for their physical, mental, emotional, and spiritual health? How does the gospel empower us to show love for our ailing parents when caring for them feels so demanding? For some seasoned couples, the weight of giving attention to the older generation is compounded by still having responsibilities for a child or two of their own living at home. They are part of the "sandwich generation," caring for both the generations ahead of them and behind them.

And importantly, how can we honor our parents without damaging our marriage? Is there some way we can maintain a strong marriage with the added strain of caring for elderly parents?

Many couples in the second half of life have found themselves caring for at least one of their parents. Maybe that's a major focus of your life right now, especially if you are in the earlier years of your second half. It's quite common for couples in their forties and fifties—and some in their sixties or even early seventies—to have living parents. Though some elderly parents die unexpectedly while still active and independent, many will slowly decline in their ability to handle life's demands, growing increasingly dependent on their family members to care for them. And the care they need broadens and deepens with the passing weeks, months, and years.

What Kind of Help Might Elderly Parents Need?

Functional help. At first, a parent might ask for your help in a small, even amusing way: *Hey, my new smartphone is smarter than I am! Can you help me figure it out?* But over time, the help required is no longer amusing. It might be downright trying to you, body and soul, as your parent needs you to assist with toileting, bathing, and getting dressed. For many couples in their second half, the need to care for elderly parents gradually escalates as the parents slowly decline in their ability to care for themselves. Other couples, though, might be suddenly thrust into the realm of elder care when a parent is stricken with a debilitating stroke or heart attack or is significantly injured in a fall. Caregiving children find themselves more and more involved in helping their mother or father with other functional needs: laundry, house cleaning, meal preparation, involvement in medical appointments, and making sure the parent's home is as safe as possible. Similar care will be needed for parents suffering from a decline into some form of dementia like Alzheimer's.

Financial help. Even if your aging parent has sufficient financial means to handle current and future expenses, they might need assistance in handling those resources. Devoting time to helping the parent pay bills and balance bank accounts might be a task you have not had previously. What about longer-term financial planning? Are you up to date on what investments or insurance policies your parent has? Do you know how to access those and other legal documents, if needed? Do you or another family member or trusted friend have power of attorney if your parent becomes unable to handle their own affairs?

Medical/health help. Does your failing parent need assistance in taking the correct medications at the proper time each day? Are they getting proper nutrition on a daily basis? What medical appointments do they have on the calendar—or need to schedule? Who will transport your parent to medical appointments? Is that person—probably a family member—able to accompany the elderly parent to that appointment, assisting in asking important questions and taking notes?

Emotional help. It's not uncommon for an elderly person to slip into significant discouragement or even depression as they realize the accumulating losses they've experienced in their season of decline. If they need your care, they have obviously lost some of their abilities and independence. Maybe they had to move from their home and feel a loss of daily familiarity. If they moved a longer distance to be closer to you or another family member, they no doubt have lost ties to their previous church and longtime friends. Most severely, they might have lost their spouse.

Spiritual help. As your elderly parent is struggling with painful losses, it's also likely they now have less-frequent contact with people who were key spiritual encouragers in their lives—close Christian friends, pastors, and former neighbors. If the aging parent is unable to participate in Sunday worship and other church gatherings, how are they getting fed spiritually? And if your parent is not yet a believer, their greatest spiritual need is to come to faith in Jesus Christ. In addition to praying for your parent's salvation, what else might you do? Might you ask your parent if they would like to hear how you came to faith in Christ? Would it be appropriate for you to ask what questions your parent has about death and the hereafter? If your parent has been quietly worrying about the end of life, they might be relieved that you are willing to open that discussion. May God pour out his grace as you have those crucial conversations.

Where Can We Find Help in Caring for Our Elderly Parents?

Reviewing just some of the needs of caring for an elderly parent feels overwhelming. Where can you find help? Take heart, my burdened friend. You are not alone. Consider the following:

The Lord is with you. He has not forgotten you. Reflect on the strength of his promise: "I will never leave you nor forsake you" (Hebrews 13:5). Even in those especially hard times, your heavenly Father knows what you are going through. He loves you. He will carry you while you are carrying the burdens of others. Are you uncertain of what decisions to make, desperately feeling your need for wisdom? Remember this encouraging reminder: "If any of you lacks wisdom, let him ask God, who gives generously to all without reproach, and it will be given him" (James 1:5).

The church family can help you. Ask friends in your small group to pray for you. It might be wise to have an agreement with your small group leader or Bible study teacher to have the freedom to pass along regular praises and requests that you and your family are facing while caring for your elderly parent. Of course, if your parent is part of a church and is still able to go to church gatherings, that is tremendously helpful. If they belong to a church but are no longer able to get to gatherings, is there a way church members could come to them? Are there people in their church—or in your church if you live nearby—who enjoy ministering to older folks? Might you arrange times for them to visit with your parent, bringing an added human touch and words of encouragement? Is it possible for one of their pastors—or one of yours—to stop by or call to share Scripture and pray with your parent? And if your parent is not yet a believer, might friends from your church be willing to show the love of Christ by coming to your home to visit not only you but also your parent? Who knows how the Lord might use your Christian friends in reaching your parent with the gospel!

What social or government agencies have resources to aid you in caring for your parent? The reason many caregivers don't access these resources is that they are unaware they exist. A good place to begin is the website for the Area Agency on Aging.[5] This not-for-profit organization has information that you can access, directing you to other resources to help you with your particular needs. This organization and others can give you information and resources that will lighten your caregiving burden.

Extended family have the privilege of coming together to help with caring for aging parents so that one person is not shouldering the responsibilities alone. Consider the implications of 1 Timothy 5:3–4: "Honor widows who are truly widows. But if a widow has children or grandchildren, let them first learn to show godliness to their own household and to make some return to their parents, for this is pleasing in the sight of God." God wants families to take care of older family members if at all possible. (See also Mark 7:9–13 for Jesus's heart for the care of parents.)

So consider your siblings, siblings-in-law, teenage or adult kids and kids-in-law, or possibly your parent's siblings who are still active and able to help in certain ways. Some caregivers carry nearly all the weight, not wanting to impose on others by asking for help. But you could use help. In addition, your parent might benefit from the added input of and interaction with other family members. And those relatives might just find themselves blessed by being included in caring for a loved one. Are there certain family members who have special training or abilities with medical issues? With finances? Are there people in your family who have more time and could help with errands or household duties? There's no harm in asking for their help, even if they are unable or unwilling to say yes.

Your spouse can help. Let me encourage the spouse of the primary caregiver to see the significant role he has. I say *he* quite deliberately, as approximately 75 percent of all caregivers are female.[6] It is often the daughter of the elderly person who has stepped up to lead the way in caring for the aging parent, though in other cases it might be the daughter-in-law. Either way, the amazing way these women serve the parent or parent-in-law should capture the respect of their husbands and inspire them to come alongside their Christ-reflecting wives in whatever way they can.

Regardless of whether the wife or the husband is the caregiver, the other spouse can lighten their load. Here are some ways you might do this:

- Look for tasks they've been doing that you can take on instead. If you don't see any, just ask.
- Offer frequent words of thanks and encouragement.
- Ask your spouse regularly what their current concerns are and how you might help.
- Take initiative in praying with them. If you are in two different locations, call to check on them, pray, and reassure them of your love.
- If the caregiving spouse is serving at the parent's home, do all you can to alleviate their concerns about the home front by taking care of the household chores, family finances, etc.

Do all this without making the caregiving spouse feel guilty by complaining about all you are doing. After all, they are likely bearing the heavier responsibility. You can reflect the love of Christ by how you gladly serve your spouse even as Christ served his bride, the church, in voluntary, sacrificial ways.

What Are Some Key Ways We Can Maintain Family Unity in Caring for an Aging Parent?

Sadly, some families are marked by relational distance and even discord. When the time comes for the "kids" to care for aging parents, the rift can become even wider. Expectations from one or more siblings that another should be the one to carry the load of caregiving, especially when that individual doesn't take initiative to help in significant ways, can hurt feelings and even encourage resentment between siblings. Ideally, caring for an elderly parent should be a loving team effort of siblings and possibly siblings-in-law.

But how does that happen? It would be wise to have a family meeting to discuss the current need for care and to explore options on how that care can be pursued. Even if the siblings and their spouses are spread out geographically, it might be possible to arrange a video call to discuss options. If the parent has the capacity and desire to be part of this conversation, arrange for them to join the meeting. Showing respect to the older generation by asking them to participate would be a gracious way forward.

Is there someone in the family who is an obvious choice to be the primary caregiver—maybe one of the siblings who lives close to the parent and has the ability to carry out this ministry? Are they willing to take on this role? How might each of the siblings contribute to meeting the needs of the parent? Are there ways the siblings-in-law can help?

If this initial conversation goes well, future family meetings can be put on the calendar to discuss how it's going and how to handle new issues that arise. If this initial meeting does not go well, especially if there is painful division among the family members on how to move forward, choosing a facilitator for the second meeting would be a wise step. A social agency, such as the Area Agency on Aging, might have a suggested moderator, or maybe a pastor would be willing to help. Above all, these choices should be bathed in prayer, asking the Lord to grant wisdom, humility, love, and unity.

How Can We Honor Our Parent with Love and Respect?

As we saw at the beginning of this chapter, God's command to "honor your father and your mother" (Exodus 20:12) has no age limit. Even if you are in your seventies and your parent is approaching one hundred years old, God still wants us to show them honor. Showing our parents honor means that we show them respect. We treat them as having the dignity and value that God created them with as his image-bearers, even if that image seems a bit clouded with physical and mental impairments. So what are some ways we can show honor to our aging parents?

By how we listen. As we have explored previously, one of the hardest aspects of people aging is the sense of loss. Over time, they have lost their previous activities, their mobility and strength, and quite likely their longtime friends and possibly even their spouse. If the aging parent speaks with a measure of pain regarding the loss of youthful vigor and meaningful relationships, we do not show honor when we respond by dismissing or minimizing the significance of their grief. How much more dignity would it communicate by entering into their pain with empathy? *That must be so hard, Mom. I can't imagine the grief you are feeling. I'm so sorry. Would you like me to pray with you about that?* This kind of response would be a wonderful reflection of Proverbs 23:22: "Listen to your father who gave you life, and do not despise your mother when she is old."

By how we speak. Especially as the degenerative effects of age take a firmer, more inclusive grip on an older person's capacities, the parent/child relationship seems to be reversed. Now it is the child who is "parenting" the parent, telling him what to do, when to do it, and how to do it. This can be humiliating to an older person. What's the alternative? We need to be careful not to nag, scold, or push our parents faster than they are ready to go, if at all possible. Instead, we should speak with patience and a calm, loving voice—even if we need to speak loudly in order to be heard!

By how we serve. There will be acts of caregiving that are difficult and humbling to give—and humiliating for the elderly loved one to receive. Put yourself in your parent's shoes. How would you feel about being dependent on someone to help you with getting dressed or undressed? Or having someone assist you with toileting? It would be hard to receive, wouldn't it? As we carry out those humbling tasks, let us do so with respect and love, not with complaining or brusqueness.

By how we bless. Family members can help bring a measure of joy and hope to a failing older person by thinking of ways to bless the family elder. Visiting is important, of course, but keep in mind that the world of the older person gets smaller and smaller as abilities and mobility shrink. They might not have a lot of new things to tell you since your last visit. Conversations can quickly become awkward.

Why not plan your visit ahead of time? Come ready to share a Scripture or to read (or sing) one of your parent's favorite hymns. My own late mother-in-law found such delight in requesting that we sing gospel songs with her, which we were glad to do.

Might you bring another family member with you? Maybe visit as a married couple or bring one of your own children or grandchildren. Bring some old photos and ask your parent to tell the story behind them, if they are able. Might your parent enjoy working on a puzzle or game that you bring, or possibly reading material they would enjoy? Another idea would be to invite one or two of your parent's friends to come with you, enjoying time to reminisce together. Wouldn't it be a delight to hear your parent laughing with an old friend?

How Can You Maintain a Healthy Marriage in This Challenging Season?

Caring for an aging parent can be draining on both body and soul. It can also be a drain on a marriage as a large measure of time, energy, and attention goes not to the spouse, but to the parent. How can a couple in the second half of life maintain a healthy marriage during this challenging season?

Because so many caregivers are women, in addition to ideas I've shared above, let me add some special counsel to the husbands. Men, some of us feel inadequate in our "husband-ing." Even though we might have been married for decades by this time of life, we can still take a way-too-passive stance toward our marriages. Now must not be a time of passivity.

We husbands always are under the gospel-centered commission to "love your wives, as Christ loved the church and gave himself up for her" (Ephesians 5:25). If our wives are giving so much of themselves in caring for their mother or father—or maybe *our* mother or father—wouldn't it honor Christ to take initiative in serving our wives in life-giving ways? How might we live out Galatians 6:2 with our wives? "Bear one another's burdens, and so fulfill the law of Christ." How might we come alongside our wives in helpful ways, not merely agreeing to do tasks when asked, but taking initiative to look for ways we can relieve some of the load they are carrying? What could we do for the elderly parent so she doesn't add that chore to her to-do list? What are the tasks we could do at our own home so she doesn't worry about finding time to squeeze in those jobs as well?

Is your wife discouraged with feelings of inadequacy, expressing, "I should have done more"? Can you affirm her value, thanking her for her admirable love as "she has done what she could" (Mark 14:8)? Is she weary physically? Can you or another relative give her a break from the elderly parent so she can have time to rest? Might you do something with her just for fun—maybe taking her on a much-needed date while someone else gives respite care? Or is she suffering from weariness of soul? Can you gently remind her of Christ's love and his gracious command, "Come to me, all who labor and are heavy laden, and I will give you rest" (Matthew 11:28), taking her hand and praying for her in her hearing?

Walking Your Parent to Heaven's Gate

The day will come when your parent passes from this life to the next. Though it is always hard to say goodbye to loved ones, what a blessing it will be to see our Christian parent off, thanking God for the privilege of walking with them on the final steps of their journey. And by God's grace, we can look forward to joining them in glory one day, having heard these words from our Master's smiling face, "Well done, good and faithful servant. You have been faithful over a little; I will set you over much. Enter into the joy of your master" (Matthew 25:21).

Are you unsure of your parent's spiritual condition? Share with them again the good news that if they will turn from their sin and put their faith in Jesus Christ, he will save them. Their response is out of our control, but we know that God is both sovereign and gracious, and we can entrust him with our parent's spiritual condition.

Questions

1. If you have parents who are getting older but are not yet in need of hands-on care, how you can be prepared when that time comes? Take some time with your spouse to make plans. If you have siblings, have a conversation with them about ways each of you might be able to serve your parents when the need arises.

2. If your parents already require care, do you feel overwhelmed by their needs? If so, which of the helps on pages 68–71 seem like the best one(s) for you to turn to first? Make a concrete plan—if possible, in conjunction with your spouse—for how you will take advantage of this source of help.

3. As you read the section on honoring your elderly parent with love and respect, what stood out to you? What would you like to change about the way you interact with your mom or dad? Pray for the grace to be able to put this change into practice.

4. If your spouse is the one actively caring for a parent, what suggestions from this chapter can you put into practice to give them the support they need? As you consider how you can help, be sure to seek input from your spouse.

Chapter 7

Investing: Becoming Intentional Biblical Grandparents Together[7]

ONE OF THE greatest delights many couples enjoy in the second half of life is having grandchildren. Their *enjoyment* level is high. But I wonder how high their *understanding* level is as grandparents. What I mean is how much time and effort have they put into trying to understand God's calling on their lives as grandparents? How much training have they received from the Bible on the ministry of grandparenting?

If you do a search on your Bible app for the word *grandparent*, you won't get many hits. However, that does not mean God's Word ignores the significant role that grandparents play in the lives of their families. The Bible does explain the mission God has given to grandparents. So what is his overarching goal? Consider the following Bible passages (emphases added):

- "Take care, and keep your soul diligently, lest you forget the things that your eyes have seen, and lest they depart from your heart all the days of your life. *Make them known to your children and your children's children*" (Deuteronomy 4:9).
- "So even to old age and gray hairs, O God, do not forsake me, *until I proclaim your might to another*

77

generation, your power to all those to come"
(Psalm 71:18).

- "*We will . . . tell to the coming generation the glorious deeds of the* LORD, *and his might, and the wonders that he has done . . . so that they should set their hope in God and not forget the works of God,* but keep his commandments" (Psalm 78:4, 7).
- "*One generation shall commend your works to another,* and shall declare your mighty acts" (Psalm 145:4).

In God's gracious providence, the torch of faith that was carried by those who preceded us was placed in our hands at some point. God wants us to be faithful in passing that torch to the coming generations. The Lord is calling on us grandparents to be diligent—to be intentional—in showing our grandchildren the greatness and grace of our glorious Lord so that they "should set their hope in God" (Psalm 78:7). Now, isn't that a worthy goal for our grandparenting—that at the end of our lives, our grandchildren will have set their hope in God? This takes intentionality.

What Does It Mean to Be Intentional as a Grandparent?

What synonyms come to your mind when you think of the word *intentional*? Maybe *purposeful*, *deliberate*, *planned*, or possibly *proactive*. If there were a "grandparent intentionality spectrum," where do you think you would land?

Perhaps on the left there might be grandparents who are not at all intentional in their grandparenting. Oh, maybe they spend time now and then with their grandkids, but their involvement is mostly reactionary. These unintentional grandparents might respond positively when asked by their kids or grandkids to do something together, but they don't *initiate* time together and they don't *plan* their involvement with the grandchildren. There's no overarching goal to their grandparenting, and no thoughtful steps planned on how to get there.

In the middle of the spectrum, where many of us find ourselves, are the grandparents who are *somewhat* intentional. These grandparents occasionally initiate meaningful interactions with their grandchildren. That's great. But what would it take to move the needle on the intentionality spectrum further to the right? What has to change for that to happen?

We can gain a good perspective on what it takes to be intentional grandparents by remembering God's directive to the people of Israel. God commanded the Israelites to intentionally pass on his Word from one generation to the next. It was for "you and your son and your son's son" (Deuteronomy 6:2). That transfer of God's Word was not a one-time event. The passing of God's truth was to be an intentional, ongoing commitment as one generation interacted with the coming generations in daily life: "These words that I command you today shall be on your heart. You shall teach them diligently to your children, and shall talk of them when you sit in your house, and when you walk by the way, and when you lie down, and when you rise" (Deuteronomy 6:6–7). That passage reminds us that we need to be intentionally using our life interactions with our grandchildren as opportunities for passing along truths about God.

Intentional Involvement in Our Grandchildren's Worlds

If we want to impact our grandchildren's lives in significant ways, we need to be intentional in building relationships with them that lead them to *want* to interact with us. To gain their love and respect, we must do what our Savior did: he entered our world and shared our life. We mirror his loving sacrifice by entering into our grandchildren's world and genuinely engaging with their lives.

Our intentional venturing into the world of grandchildren can start in their earliest days, even while they are babies and toddlers. We grandparents can make our homes not only a safe place for the grandbabies but also a welcoming place. How encouraging it would be to our kids when they realize we've been intentional in preparing our home for the grand-children's visit in order to make their visit more inviting. While we don't have to go overboard, how much money and effort would it take for us to have some key baby items in our homes?

As the grandchildren get older, we can continue to be intentional in making our home a fun place for them, pro-viding a place where they *want* to be—where they can make memories with their grandparents. Having some age-appropriate toys, games, and outdoor activities can commu-nicate to our grandchildren and their parents that we have been anticipating their visits and take delight in preparing for them. Maybe you still have some of your own kids' favorite toys and games tucked away in an attic or closet. What fun to tell your grandchildren, "Your Daddy/Mommy loved to play with this!"

Of course, as intentionally engaged grandparents, we don't want to automatically send the grandkids off by themselves to play so that we can continue our own preferred activities. As much as possible, we want to spend time *with* our grandkids. When we have that imaginary tea party, kick the ball around in the backyard, or make engine noises while we push the toy car around, we intentionally engage in our grandchildren's world, building warm relationships and making lasting memories.

As the grandchildren move into their school-age years, we grandparents can be intentional in making sure we know when their various school and extracurricular activities are scheduled. If possible, we can attend their athletic games, their musical or theatrical productions, or their school's open house.

We can encourage our grandchildren by telling them ahead of time that we're looking forward to being there, then praising their involvement in the activity. Maybe we want to celebrate afterward by taking the family out for a special treat. Doing so might become a memorable tradition for your family.

Of course, due to distance, health, or work responsibilities, grandparents can't always attend their grandchildren's activities. But there are still ways to be intentionally engaged in our grandchildren's world. By putting our grandkids' scheduled activities on our calendars, we can make a phone call beforehand, asking them how they are feeling about their upcoming event, expressing our regrets that we can't be there, and maybe even praying for them over the phone. We could ask one of the parents to send photos or a recording of the event, allowing you to make a follow-up call afterward to celebrate and encourage them. The key is intentionality—communicating to your grandchildren by your words and actions that they are on your mind and in your heart.

Intentionally Inviting Our Grandchildren into Our World

With. It's such a simple word, but it can denote such power— such potential. Think about Luke's observation in Acts 4:13, "When they saw the boldness of Peter and John, and perceived that they were uneducated, common men, they were astonished. And they recognized that they had been *with* Jesus" (emphasis added). The religious leaders were amazed at the boldness of these common men and connected the dots that the power demonstrated in the lives of these former fishermen came from their having been "with Jesus." Jesus had impacted them by his life and teaching. They were changed by being with Jesus. Reflecting our Lord, we grandparents can invite our grandchildren to walk through life *with* us. We can invite them into our world so they can learn more about life and eternity.

Think of the possibilities. Though the primary responsibility for training and discipling the children rests with their parents, we grandparents can come alongside and have life-changing influence on our grandchildren. What if we grandparents developed an intentional "with" approach to ordinary daily activities, deliberately including our grandchildren whenever possible, demonstrating for them and coaching them in helpful life skills? It might be as simple as coaching a preschooler on where to place the napkin as you are preparing the table for a family meal, or teaching an older child how to bake cookies or fix a leaky faucet or do the grocery shopping. Wouldn't it be helpful for grandparents to teach their grandchildren how to shake hands when they meet an adult, or to include them in putting gas in the car and teaching them some safety points in the process?

As the children grow, their ability to engage in daily responsibilities and chores grows too. Helping our grandchild learn how to ride a bike morphs—overnight, it seems—into helping them learn how to drive a car. However we do it, we can assist our adult children in the amazing responsibility of preparing our grandchildren for life by doing life *with* our grandchildren. This mindset can provide increased opportunities to impact their lives for God's glory, helping shape them for life and eternity.

Intentionally Pursuing Adventures with Our Grandchildren

If our heartfelt, prayerful desire for our grandchildren is that they become fully devoted followers of Jesus Christ, why would we encourage them to pursue a lifestyle of safety, ease, and comfort? Life is not centered on us. Life is centered on Jesus Christ, and following him is costly. Jesus says, "If anyone would come after me, let him deny himself and take up his cross daily and follow me. For whoever would save his life will lose it, but whoever loses his life for my sake will save it" (Luke 9:23–24).

Without being harsh, we grandparents can inspire our grandchildren to "do hard things for God." Pioneer missionary to India William Carey is often quoted as saying, "Expect great things from God; attempt great things for God." What might be some things we grandparents can do to influence our grandchildren to attempt great things for God over the course of their lifetimes?

Clearly, we must pray for more than our grandchildren's safety and comfort in life. We want to intentionally pray that the Spirit of God will move in their hearts in such a way that they will want to be "all in" for Christ and the spread of his gospel. We can model a lifestyle that shows that *our* ultimate goal in life is not our own comfort or safety but the spread of the glory of Christ in the world.

This commitment in our lives will be evident not only by what we talk about but also by how we use our time, our money, and our possessions. Do our grandchildren see us using the bulk of our time in pursuing our own pleasures, or do they see us investing a significant portion of our time serving our local church or helping in a local ministry? Do they see Grandpa and Grandma indulging themselves with their money, or do they see us investing in God's kingdom through sacrificial giving? Do our grandchildren see us being protective of our possessions, or do they see us mirroring Christ's generosity by gladly lending our things and opening up our home in gracious hospitality? Our grandchildren are watching us. What do they see?

As grandparents, let's do some honest evaluation of the example we're setting for our grandchildren. Wouldn't it be glorious if our grandchildren would grow up with memories of grandparents who intentionally communicate by example as well as by counsel, *Let's live radically for Jesus. He is worth it!*

Intentionally Engage Your Grandchildren in Meaningful Conversation

What do we tend to talk about with our grandchildren? A lot depends on their age and situation. But no matter if our grandchild is eight or eighteen, are the majority of our conversations meaningful? Are we thoughtfully processing life with our grandchildren in our interactions with them, whether those conversations are happening face to face, on the phone, or through social media?

I wonder how much we could improve our conversations with our grandchildren through the simple step of intentionally asking more significant questions. For example, instead of asking your grandchild, "Did you enjoy school today?" (a yes/no question), you could ask a more significant open-ended question such as "What was the biggest challenge you faced at school today?" or "What was a blessing you experienced today?" Those questions could surface all kinds of opportunities to lean into your grandkid's world, exploring their concerns, offering comfort, encouraging them, and exploring ways the gospel might relate to their situations.

Having these kinds of conversations with our grandchildren might require growth in our own patterns of how we relate to others. I am still learning to be less self-focused, more curious about others, and a better listener. We can change. We can grow. If we are true followers of Jesus Christ, we have the Holy Spirit in our lives. He can and does change us. So let's ask him, *Please, Lord, help me to be less focused on myself and 'do nothing from selfish ambition or conceit, but in humility count others more significant' than myself* (Philippians 2:3).

As we grow in Christlike regard for others, we can intentionally initiate conversations with our grandchildren on spiritually significant issues. For example, if our grandchildren are part of a church, we might ask them, "What did you learn in Sunday school (or in youth group or from the pastor's sermon)?" Maybe we then explore that passage or topic with the child for a few minutes, looking for its meaning and impact on the child's life. Or perhaps we can welcome our grandchild into our own spiritual life: "Guess what I was reading in my Bible this morning. I was reading . . . and do you know what that got me thinking about?" And the conversation develops, not only about the words on the page but also about the impact of God's Word on your life personally.

Discussing the Bible personally with our grandchildren demonstrates for them its power in our own lives. These conversations of the Bible's impact on our lives can be a gracious way to open spiritual discussions with our grandchildren who are not growing up with believing parents. They might not have the opportunity to hear teaching from God's Word from their parents, making spiritual input from us all the more significant in their young lives. When grandchildren are old enough to read, we can encourage them to read the Bible on their own or with us. Having conversations together about Scripture can allow us to process what they're reading, asking them how a passage impacted them or what questions it stirred.

Your grandchild might be facing a painful time in his life that you need to process with him—hurts from the death of a friend or family member, moving to a new community, or the separation of his parents. When our grandchildren are struggling with their own sin or the pain of being sinned against, we can process that pain and confusion with them. We don't serve our grandchildren by minimizing their pain. Instead, let's listen to their pain and struggles, drawing out their hearts. This might mean gently asking questions, being quiet with them, even crying with them. And it will mean going to God with them in prayer.

We grandparents can be a safe place for our grandchildren to talk openly about their questions, doubts, struggles, and hurts. Let's determine ahead of time that, by God's grace, we will humbly and lovingly engage them where they are. At times, we might feel at a loss to know what to say, but let's ask the Lord to fill us with his Spirit, giving us the wisdom and loving sensitivity to be present and to know what to say and what not to say.

Intentionally Affirming Our Grandchildren

There are so many ways we can intentionally affirm our grandchildren and reassure them of our love. Nothing beats saying the words, *I love you, buddy* or *I love you, sweetheart.* Some of us grew up never hearing those sweet words from our own grandparents or parents. But by God's empowering grace, we can reflect his love for us by regularly verbalizing to our grandchildren, "I love you!"

We can demonstrate our love for our grandchildren through appropriate affection—hugs and kisses. If you grew up not being shown proper physical affection, showing affection to your own family members might feel awkward. But isn't it worth overcoming our hesitations for the sake of letting our grandchildren know how much we love them?

Intentionally affirming our grandchildren through appropriate words of praise can make an impact as well. We can ask the Lord to help us identify and communicate his gifts of kindness and grace to our grandchildren. The praise we give should not ignore God's involvement, but instead draw attention to him. For example, if you have an academically gifted grandchild, it would be so easy to brag, "You sure are smart!" But how much more meaningful to say, "You know, it seems that God has given you an unusual ability to learn. I'm praying that you will use that ability to serve God and to bless others"? Similar things might be said to a grandchild who has accomplished something notable in athletics or the arts. And how encouraging it would be for a grandparent to affirm a grandson or granddaughter who has excelled in serving others or showing compassion to someone in need.

Let's intentionally look for those evidences of God's grace to, and through, our grandchild, then point out that virtue or ability in a way that acknowledges the God who gave that blessing.

Providing the Legacy of a Long Marriage

If we as married couples in the second half of life have been gripped by God's saving and sanctifying grace, many of us have something precious to offer our grandchildren: the legacy of a marriage that has leaned on God's grace and thrived over the years. We can show our grandkids the very meaning and purpose of marriage by how we live as a long-married couple. We have lived long enough together to know from God's Word that marriage was never designed to be self-centered. Marriage is for our spouse and for Christ. Marriage is a mission shared by husband and wife of showing a watching world a reflection of the greatest love story ever—the love that Christ has for his bride, the church (Ephesians 5:22–33).

Over the years, we have encountered struggles and trials, but by God's sustaining grace, our marriage has persevered and we can serve as living examples of God's sustaining, empowering grace to the coming generations. Yes, let us leave the legacy of a long marriage for the glory of Christ and the good of the next generation.

Perhaps your marriage is not as long as that of some of your peers due to death or divorce, then remarriage. Rather than feeling discouraged that you are not leaving a legacy of a long marriage, you can find joy in being able to tell your own story. You can share with your kids and grandkids the story of God's grace in helping you journey through your pain and grief, bringing you fresh opportunities to reflect Christ's love with your new spouse. Your legacy is also a gift, blessing the next generation with the story of God's faithfulness in your life and inspiring them to trust him more.

Questions

1. Where would you place yourself on the "grandparent intentionality spectrum"? Consider the material in this chapter and pray about how it might help you in your grandparenting. What would it look like to begin doing, or do more of, or do differently some of the topics we explored? Discuss with your spouse ways you can encourage each other as you seek to become more intentional grandparents.

2. Review the various ways grandparents can be part of their grandchildren's worlds. For suggestions that are tailored to your own grandchildren, reach out to their parents. Pray about what you can do. Then take a first step to enter more fully into your grandchildren's lives.

3. Think about the kinds of things you pray for your grandchildren. Has this chapter given you new ideas of meaningful ways to pray for them? If so, take time now to pray in that new way.

Chapter 8

Refocusing: Exploring Purposeful Retirement

OF THE MANY transitions in the second half of life, few are weightier than retirement. Some of you have already been retired for a season. How is it going so far? For others, retirement still seems elusively far off—especially on your harder days at work. How much longer will it be before you can leave your current employment? Most people in North America are retired by their mid-sixties.

Thinking about retirement raises some practical questions. The two most commonly asked questions about retirement are *When can I retire?* and *Can I afford it?* But there are a host of other questions we should ask: *What's the purpose of retirement?*, *What am I going to do with my freed-up time?*, *Should I look for another career or maybe a part-time job after I retire?*, *How is retirement going to impact our marriage?*, and most importantly, *What does God's Word say about retirement?*

How Are We Christians to Think About Retirement?

The common understanding of *retire* is "to leave your job or stop working," especially if you have reached a certain age. Why would someone stop working at their place of gainful employment? There are a variety of possible reasons. Some people retire because they must. Maybe they experience a sudden health crisis that propels them unexpectedly into the realm of retirement. For another person, the health concerns were not suddenly thrust upon them but overtook them gradually, leaving them physically, mentally, and/or emotionally unable to adequately do the job they were hired to perform. They just know, *It's time to quit. I can't do this anymore.*

There are some people, such as commercial pilots, military personnel, first responders, etc., who face a mandatory retirement age, even if they would love to continue on. Others choose to retire even if they could stay on. Maybe they are just tired of the stress of their current employment: long hours, demanding deadlines, an unreasonable boss, an irritating coworker, too many work-related travels, or a wearisome daily commute. Or maybe it's the realization that they can finally afford to walk away and spend their freed-up time doing "me" things.

Here are a few important questions that would be good to process as a married couple in the second half of life: If retirement is walking away from your job, what are you walking *toward*? What are you retiring *to*?

For the last few generations, our culture has sought to sell us on the idea that we are to retire to a life of leisure. We are encouraged to work hard at our jobs for decades, saving up for retirement. And what are we supposed to do with that money we put toward our nest egg? Spend it on ourselves! Enough sacrificing. Now is the time to do what *you* want to do. What might that be? Well, that's up to you, but there are plenty of advertisements to entice you to spend your savings on moving to a retirement community in warmer climes or building that hideaway in the mountains. Just think of all the ways you can spend your time and money on "me" activities as you vacation fifty-two weeks a year! Wouldn't that be living "the American dream" at last?

But the American dream that is pitched to us in the second half of life turns out to be not so much of a dream after all. It's more like a mirage. For many people who have worked for hourly wages over the decades, it seems they have not been able to save enough money to afford this supposed life of leisure in their older years. And for many professionals and others who found they *could* afford to purchase this American dream, the promised delight they were sold soon left them with buyer's remorse. Somehow, playing one more round of golf or one more game of pickleball, finding one more seashell, buying one more article of clothing, or trying one more restaurant just wasn't doing it. They begin to wonder, *What could we do next?* But the joy of doing the next thing eventually dulls as well. What's the alternative?

What Is the Bible's Teaching on Work?

Retirement is "ceasing from work." But does God really want us to not work at all? Let's start at the beginning. In the very first chapter of our Bibles, we read this: "Then God said, 'Let us make man in our image, after our likeness. And let them have dominion over the fish of the sea and over the birds of the heavens and over the livestock and over all the earth and over every creeping thing that creeps on the earth'" (Genesis 1:26). "Having dominion" implies work—the work of managing or ruling the nonhuman creation for God's glory and the good of that creation.

In Genesis 2:15, we see this picture of God's purpose for Adam, his image-bearer: "The LORD God took the man and put him in the garden of Eden to work it and keep it." Did you catch that? "To work it and keep it." Let's not miss that this commission from God to humans was *before* the fall into sin (described in chapter 3). Work is not the result of sin and the curse it brought. Work has been a key part of God's design for us image-bearers from the very beginning—working for his glory and the good of his creation.

Let's go to the other end of our Bibles. How will we redeemed people be spending eternity? My friend, we will not be sitting on clouds playing harps all the livelong day. In the very last chapter of our Bibles, we read this brief description of our commission in eternity: "They will reign forever and ever" (Revelation 22:5). Whoa! This last page reminds us of something we read on the first page—that description of Adam and Eve being made in God's image to "have dominion" over creation. Human beings were designed by God from the beginning to work for his glory, and we will spend eternity carrying out that mission.

I wish I could see your face right now. Does that brief description of working in eternity excite you or depress you? If it's the latter, I understand. Work can be hard. It has been hard ever since Adam and Eve sinned, bringing God's curse upon this created order. What did God say to our ultimate ancestor, Adam?

> "Because you have listened to the voice of your wife and have eaten of the tree of which I commanded you, 'You shall not eat of it,' cursed is the ground because of you; in pain you shall eat of it all the days of your life; thorns and thistles it shall bring forth for you; and you shall eat the plants of the field. By the sweat of your face you shall eat bread, till you return to the ground, for out of it you were taken; for you are dust, and to dust you shall return." (Genesis 3:17–19)

Just think about those words from the Creator about work ever since Adam sinned: *cursed, pain, thorns and thistles, sweat,* and eventually, death itself. Work can be hard, even frustrating. Work doesn't always work, does it?

Need some encouragement? It won't always be this way. One day, Jesus will return and he will lift the curse (Revelation 22:3). Our eternal work will once again be curse-free. We will feel no more frustration but full and free delight in our eternal work of ruling the created order under our King's leadership and for our King's glory.

In the meantime, what is God's intention for us as his redeemed people? Ephesians 2:10 explains to us, "For we are his workmanship, created in Christ Jesus for good works, which God prepared beforehand, that we should walk in them." God created and redeemed us to work for his glory and the good of others. Jesus says, "Let your light shine before others, so that they may see your good works and give glory to your Father who is in heaven" (Matthew 5:16). What a privilege to live and work in a Spirit-powered way that points others to the inestimable treasure of our Lord. Jesus Christ "gave himself for us to redeem us from all lawlessness and to purify for himself a people for his own possession who are zealous for good works" (Titus 2:14).

If we buy into the world's lie that the best thing in retirement is to live for ourselves—for our own leisurely pleasures—we will be making much of ourselves and little of Christ. But we want to make much of him—to demonstrate to those witnessing our pursuits and preferences that Jesus is to be treasured above everything this world has to offer. So how do we do that in our retirement years?

Choosing a Life of Honoring God and Blessing Others by a Fruitful Retirement

Being duped by the world's snake-oil sales pitch that we should pursue a self-centered, self-gratifying retirement of ease ends up disappointing us as God's people, distracting others from the Greatest Treasure, and dishonoring our Lord. What is a better lifestyle for our retirement years? Consider these encouraging words from Psalm 92:12–15: "The righteous flourish like the palm tree and grow like a cedar in Lebanon. They are planted in the house of the LORD; they flourish in the courts of our God. They still bear fruit in old age; they are ever full of sap and green, to declare that the LORD is upright; he is my rock, and there is no unrighteousness in him." Still bearing fruit in old age—now *there's* something to aspire to in retirement.

What Might a Fruitful Life in Retirement Look Like?

A key word to guide us in considering how we might live fruitful lives in our older years is *calling*. What do you believe God is calling you to in this season of life as a married couple? The answer will vary from person to person and couple to couple, and it will even morph as you continue to make your journey through your second half of life.

For example, in your active years of retirement, you might still have the vigor to help build houses for Habitat for Humanity or go with a mission team to a developing nation. By your declining years, you might not be doing physically strenuous ministries, but rocking babies in your church's nursery or reading the Bible aloud to visually impaired residents at a nursing home would suit you just fine.

Once you find yourself dependent on others to do normal, daily tasks, you might think your years of fruitfulness are behind you, but maybe they are not. Might you volunteer to be one of your church's "prayer warriors," or might you have a ministry of writing encouraging notes or texting daily Bible verses to your grandkids and great-grandkids?

The point is, the fruit you bear might look different as you advance in age, but until the Lord calls you home or renders you fully disabled, you can still be fruitful.

So where do you start in discerning God's calling on you to serve him by serving others in your retirement years? It might be wise to dedicate extended time to think about this life-directing question, especially if you have recently stepped away from a demanding career. You need time with your spouse to slow down, pray, talk, listen, and discern God's leading as you enter a significantly new season of life. Some spiritual advisors recommend taking a sabbatical of weeks or months for this purpose soon after you step away from employment. Regardless, consider taking these steps together during that time:

Pray together. As husband and wife, go to the throne of God as his much-loved children to "present your bodies as a living sacrifice, holy and acceptable to God, which is your spiritual worship" (Romans 12:1). Tell him of your desire to live for his glory rather than your own. Ask him to give you fruitfulness in your retirement years.

Talk as a couple. Is your spouse struggling with their identity now that they're no longer in their previous vocation? Listen to them. Lean in with compassion, and gently remind them of *whose* they are. They are a child of the Most High God, even if they are no longer in a role they enjoyed for years. Or is your spouse concerned about having enough money to make it through your retirement years? Don't minimize their concerns but maximize trust in your heavenly Father's loving provision for you as his children (Matthew 6:25–33).

Consider the needs of the people closest to you. Do you and your spouse have a parent who is in failing health and needs assistance? Is one of your adult children going through particularly hard times, or even just very busy times? How might your grandchildren benefit from your increased, intentional involvement in their lives? Or maybe your own spouse needs your time and attention more than ever right now. Don't overlook your own family as you consider ways to use your freed-up time for God's glory and the good of others.

Consider the ministry needs in your church and community. Do you have time to help? Do you and/or your spouse have work experience or spiritual gifts that would help to meet that need? Talk to each other as a married couple. Do you sense the Lord's leading in a particular direction? Is he giving you a passion to get involved in a specific ministry? Explore how you might volunteer to help.

Consider your financial status. Though you might not be employed full-time any longer, do you need to work part-time to make ends meet or to add to your less-than-ideal savings account as you prepare for the future? Could you find a job that would give you not only an income but also opportunities to represent Christ there?

Does Devoting Our Retirement to Serving God by Serving Others Mean It's Wrong to Rest?

One reason many people look forward to retirement is that they are tired—tired of the stresses of a demanding boss, tight deadlines, or the feeling of not being appreciated. The idea of being retired—sleeping in, doing activities you really enjoy, being your own boss—sounds very inviting. So does this proposal that we see our retirement years as an opportunity to serve God by serving people in fruitful ways sound too demanding?

It's not wrong to want to rest. Rest is a biblical concept. Even God himself "rested on the seventh day from all his work that he had done" (Genesis 2:2). God wants us to rest. He built a need for rest into us physically, mentally, emotionally, and spiritually. Resting from our labors is a way of reminding ourselves that the world doesn't need us for it to keep on spinning. We can go to sleep at night knowing God never slumbers nor sleeps (Psalm 121:4). Resting reminds us of God's trustworthiness and our dependence on him.

As our bodies age, our energy level decreases and the aches and pains increase. Yes, we want to live fruitful lives to the glory of God as we serve others in our retirement, but we

get tired. We need rest more often and maybe in bigger incre-
ments, and that's okay. So take naps to the glory of God when
you need to! Take some days off after a particularly tiring
event. Schedule an occasional sabbatical to refresh your body
and soul. Learning to rest can actually prolong your years of
service and make your life more enjoyable in the process.

How Can We Have a Healthy Marriage in Our Retirement Years?

Next to financial concerns, one of the most commonly
expressed concern as people near retirement is the health
of their marriage. Especially if the husband and wife have
drifted apart during the busyness of their employment years,
the idea of being together 24/7 might seem scary. Each individual has gotten used to doing his/her own thing for a major
portion of every week, and now they are going to be together
nearly all the time. What are they going to do with their
time? What are they going to do with each other? Will their
retirement years be filled with the frustration of having their
spouse always around, doing things the "wrong" way or at
the "wrong" time?

You will need God's grace, and God gives grace to the
humble. So humble yourself before God, confessing your
fears and asking for his help. Humble yourself before your
spouse, expressing your concern for the future and asking
for a heart-to-heart conversation. Rather than being content
with a distant relationship, look at your newfound flexible
schedules as an opportunity to pursue one another as perhaps
you haven't in years. Without any screens in front of you, talk
as you eat meals together, take walks, and travel in the car.
Working together on your budget, list of weekly chores, and
family calendar can be bonding exercises if done with grace
and patience. Over time, as you continue your fruitful journey
together in your second half of life, you might feel as if you're

on a long second honeymoon, seeing your spouse not only as a lover but also as your best friend.

Questions

1. What vision of retirement have you had? Has this chapter in any way challenged that vision? If so, how?
2. If you have already retired, how has that experience been so far? Discuss your answer with your spouse, intently listening to their response as well.
3. If you have not yet retired, what changes do you anticipate retirement will bring? Discuss your answer with your spouse, intently listening to their response as well.
4. Take time with your spouse to talk through the questions raised in the section *What Might a Fruitful Life in Retirement Look Like?*

Chapter 9

Serving: Finding Ways to Serve Together in Our Seasoned Years

THE SECOND HALF of life has some significant milestones, doesn't it? As we have already seen, two significant stages are entering the empty nest years and moving into retirement. At these milestones, we encounter crossroads. Will we take *this* road or *that* road? Choosing the path ahead should compel us to slow down—maybe even stop—to check our spiritual GPS. We could just naively barrel ahead without much consideration for which is the better way, but that could lead to frustration or even disaster down the road. Where are we going, anyway? What's our destination in life—our *ultimate* destination?

The old maxim *Start with the end in view* is good advice for living a purposeful, fruitful life. For years, I've told those closest to me, "I want to live my life for that One, that day, and those words." What do I mean? *That One* is Jesus Christ. *That day* refers to that day I stand before him, either at my death or his return, to give an account of my life. *Those words* points me to the hope of hearing his gracious commendation on that day: "Well done, good and faithful servant" (Matthew 25:21). If that's my intended destination, what road do I take to get there? What road do we take as a married couple in the second half of our lives?

Encountering the milestones of the empty nest or retirement can bring a measure of sadness—the end of a significant season of our lives. But it can also bring a burst of joy—even unexpected giddiness—to a couple in the second half of life. *We're free, free at last! All those years of pouring into our kids and our jobs are behind us. Now it's time for us!*

But as we discussed in the previous chapter, the dazzle of "me time" tends to dull after a while. The excitement we enjoy in those earlier miles going down the "me" road wears off. We begin to hope for some new experience around the next corner that might resurrect the lost luster of the "me" road. What's wrong? What's missing?

Let's pause our journey and evaluate where we're going, why we're going there, and how we'll reach our destination.

What Is Our Collective Mission as Image-Bearers?

It's good to live with the end in view—our ultimate destination. But it's also helpful to live with the beginning in view—what were we created for? Why do we exist? What was God's purpose in creating us? Let's explore further what we learned in the previous chapter about God's plan. God commissioned us image-bearers—the pinnacles of his creation—to "be fruitful and multiply and fill the earth and subdue it" (Genesis 1:28).

The mission God gave his image-bearers has two parts. First, "fill" the earth and second, "subdue" the earth. Both parts of this mission require a team—a husband-and-wife team. Filling the earth with additional image-bearers would be impossible for Adam to accomplish on his own. That's pretty obvious, isn't it? That's one reason God said, "It is not good that the man should be alone; I will make him a helper fit for him" (Genesis 2:18). God created marriage so the married couple could carry out their mission of having children who would have children who would have children—filling the earth with image-bearers of the glorious Creator God.

The second part of the mission—"subduing" the earth—is best done as a team too. God wanted Adam and Eve to work together as a married couple to manage the earth, devoting themselves to making the world around them thrive for the glory of God. Adam and Eve had purpose. God had given them a mission that focused on more than themselves.

So what does that have to do with us? Well, God has never withdrawn the mission statement he gave the first couple. Generations later, we are still commissioned to bring God glory in filling the earth and subduing it.

You might have had children—but that's not the end of your role in God's commission. We're all still involved in filling the earth with God's glory as we evangelize and disciple other image-bearers, including our own kids and grandkids. And we are still under commission to subdue this earth, being called to work together as a husband and wife in helping other people and creation itself thrive for God's glory. Yes, we are still on mission as a married couple, and that mission goes beyond pursuing our own pleasures in the second half of life. So let us choose the way ahead carefully, thoughtfully, and intentionally.

What Is Your Particular Mission as a Married Couple?

Let's say you are embracing this significant concept of serving in ministry together as a married couple in the second half of life. Though you might feel a bit of anxiety—there are so many unknowns—you are intrigued. You're wondering, *How might God use us in this next season of our lives and marriage?* How do you decide what God's specific calling on you two might be? Here are some steps to guide you:

Pray. As a couple, ask the Lord for his guidance. Be encouraged. Remember, the Holy Spirit graciously gives gifts to members of the body of Christ (1 Corinthians 12:11). And the Holy Spirit empowers believers for ministry (Acts 4:8, 31; Acts 6:3, 5; Ephesians 5:18). So with these hope-fueling reminders from the Bible, ask the Lord to give you a united awareness of a ministry need and lead you as a couple to the path of service he wants you to travel together.

Process. Talk openly as a couple. Share your thoughts and passions with your spouse. With humility, listen to each other's ideas. Respond to each other's contributions with encouraging affirmation. Explore the possibilities by asking the following questions:

- *Whom is the Lord calling you to serve?* Start close to home. How about your own kids and grandkids, siblings, or nieces and nephews? What about your local church? Think about your community. And is the Lord inviting you to make some contribution to his work in the world at large?
- *Where might God be calling you to as a married couple?* Look around. Again, don't miss the possible ministries to those closest to you: your own kids, grandkids, and other family members. If the Lord has given you more flexible time than you've had in the past, does he want you to devote some time to intentionally pour into your family for God's glory and their eternal good? Are there existing ministries in your local church that could use your help? Do you see gaps in your church's ministry that you might fill? Has the Lord given you a passion for an existing ministry in your community that would gladly welcome your involvement: the crisis pregnancy center, Meals on Wheels, a homeless shelter, or food pantry, etc.? Is there another local need you could help with,

such as helping with your church's landscaping or driving seniors to their doctor's appointments? Just think of the possible ministries you two could serve in!

- *What specific ways has the Lord prepared you for a particular ministry as a couple?* What spiritual gifts has the Lord given you? What have you heard from your spouse and others regarding your giftedness? What do you see as your spouse's primary gifts? Have you told them? Do they agree with your observations? Do you or your spouse have life experiences that might be useful in a particular way? We often think of traditional church ministry such as teaching or music, but don't limit your thinking as you evaluate where God might use you. Do you have special training from a previous job or from a longtime hobby? How might those skills be useful for the glory of God and the good of people? What about the passions God has given you and your spouse? Do you care deeply about certain needs or situations that you would love to help with? And let's not miss a ministry you can do together that has so much potential for blessing others: the ministry of hospitality. Romans 12:13 directs all of us to "seek to show hospitality." The words *seek to show* actually translate one word in the original Greek: *pursue.* Think about that for a minute: *pursue* hospitality. Go after it, looking for people you could bless through your ministry of hospitality: friends and neighbors who don't know Christ, people new to your church, small group Bible studies, younger couples who might benefit from your example as a seasoned married couple, etc. If your current living arrangement isn't conducive to inviting people into your home, could you ask others to join you at a restaurant or at a local park for a picnic? Think creatively!

- *When could you start?* Are there certain ministries you would like to help with and are ready to jump into? Or does this potential field of ministry need a fair amount of prayer and planning before you and your spouse are ready to launch? Do you need to get more training or go through a qualification process before you can get involved in a particular ministry you felt led to pursue? When can you start preparing?

- *Why do you want to serve in this way?* Lord willing, you are already following the biblical call on married couples to live missionally. That's wonderful. Also think about why you want to pursue serving in this particular way. Let me encourage you. On one hand, we should be willing to jump in and serve to meet any need that we become aware of. For most of us, the years we spent caring for our kids when they were growing up taught us that. I don't recall ever meeting a parent who said they felt "gifted" in cleaning up a baby with a major diaper blowout, yet that unpleasant task had to be done. So yes, be willing to do whatever really needs to be done. But when you have a choice in how you serve, there's nothing wrong with gravitating to ministries that you really enjoy. I have found that people who are gifted by the Spirit in specific ways find their batteries getting charged when they do that ministry. The "enjoyment factor" often leads to glad longevity and fruitfulness in that ministry of giftedness. On the other hand, spending too much time in nongifted areas tends to drain people's batteries, eventually moving them to keep glancing at the exit, looking for an opportunity to leave without too much embarrassment. I propose that this principle lies behind Peter's exhortation in 1 Peter 4:10–11: "As each has received a gift, use it to serve one another, as good stewards of God's varied grace: whoever speaks, as one who speaks oracles of God; whoever serves, as one who serves by the strength that God supplies—in order that in everything God may be glorified through Jesus Christ. To him belong glory and dominion forever and ever. Amen."

Plunge in! If there is a current need for a particular ministry and you and your spouse feel ready to begin, why not get started? Think of the shared joy you and your spouse can experience as you bless others in your ministry together.

But what do you do if you or your spouse still have some hesitations—some *what ifs*? Let's deal with some of those next.

Working Through the What Ifs

What if my spouse and I don't have time to get involved in a ministry together? Some couples in the second half of their marriage truly have schedules that are overflowing due to a demanding career(s) or having an unusually challenging family situation—or both. But for most people who have already entered the empty-nest years—and possibly even their retirement years—it would be helpful to take a hard look at the weekly schedule and ask, "What are we so busy with?" Are there some activities that could be set aside so you can get more involved in a fruitful ministry with your spouse? It's worth an honest, unhurried look at your calendar together, isn't it? Even if you find only a little space on your calendar, consider getting involved in a not-too-demanding ministry together, knowing that one day your lives might not be as busy as they are now.

What if my spouse and I have significantly different gifts, personalities, and passions? That's quite possible, but that doesn't necessarily preclude enjoying serving in a ministry together. For example, sometimes one spouse is an extrovert, thriving on interacting with other people. The other spouse is more of an introvert, much preferring to serve behind the scenes. You could still use your gifts in a complementary way, with one of you being the "front" person who interacts with others while the other cares for many of the support needs for the ministry?

For us, both my wife, Gladine, and I can teach. For me, public speaking still charges my batteries after decades of serving in that capacity. For Gladine, preparing a lesson for a seminar session requires lots of prep time—and a little help from her husband. On the other hand, Gladine exudes care and sensitivity to others in one-on-one conversations and smaller group settings. I don't think I come across nearly as warmly in those situations. So when I travel to speak at a conference or seminar, people love it when Gladine comes with me. They seek her out during break times and small group discussions, knowing their hearts will be warmed from the interaction they have with her. Even though our gifts are not the same, they complement one another. Could you and your spouse find a similar arrangement of serving together with complementary gifts and passions?

What if we can't keep doing the same ministry over the years ahead? Good question. Life over the course of the second half is not uniform, is it? It's likely that many folks in the early days of their second half are still quite active. Over time, though, they experience a gradual decline in energy and mobility. Unless we die suddenly, nearly all of us will notice ourselves slowing down a bit with each additional birthday candle. Then the time comes when we find ourselves dependent on others to do basic tasks that we used to do for ourselves. That latter season of life can be marked by disability and dependence.

So how do we think through this commitment to ministry in the second half of life? Eventually, we all realize *This is a whole lot harder to do than it used to be*, or *I can't do that anymore*. But let me encourage you that while we might be saddened by our diminishing ministry abilities, we don't need to assume that our years of ministry are over. They've just changed. We can still be "on mission," just in different ways. Though one day we might not have the physical or mental capacity to do demanding ministry, we can ask the Lord to show us what we *can* do.

Let me tell you a story. Gladine and I grew up in the same church, and one time she and I visited a nursing home to see one of the Sunday school teachers we had as children. This teacher had been an amazing woman in her earlier years, devoting so much time to evangelizing and teaching children. Now, decades later, she was in a wheelchair, no longer able to do the ministries she so much enjoyed over the previous decades. But we didn't hear her complaining about the loss of her earlier ministry. Instead, she related to us how she devoted much of her time to prayer. She told us that she had prayed for *us* every day for years!

Gladine and I later pondered if some of the fruit of our ministry labors was actually God's answer to *her* prayers for us. Even if the breadth of our ministry diminishes as we age, the depth can increase as we devote our remaining energy to praying for others. And in our more feeble years, we can still intentionally bless others through gospel-fueled, Christ-exalting words of encouragement during visits from family and friends and through notes we send their way.

The Ministry of Modeling the Legacy of a Long Marriage

Many younger people have seen the marriages of people in their lives fall apart. Sometimes, the breakup of a family member's marriage—maybe their parents'—has impacted them very personally. It's not too surprising to encounter younger people who are cynical about marriage, wondering if matrimony is worth the effort. Others are fearful, questioning if they have what it takes to have a long marriage when people close to them have divorced.

If by God's grace we've been married for decades, a key ministry we have (but maybe haven't given enough thought to) is providing the legacy of a long marriage. When we live as a gladly married older couple before our kids, our grandkids, younger singles, and married folks in our local churches, the very fact that we're still married after all these years can inspire them with life-giving hope.

Lord willing, they will come to see the effectiveness of the gospel in the marriage of two imperfect people, gripped and united by God's perfect love. They will begin to smell the sweet aroma of Christ (2 Corinthians 2:14) in our marriage, leading them away from the cynicism they have gotten from the stench of this broken, fallen world. And if we are willing to live humbly and openly before them, we can invite them into our lives as a long-married couple, telling the story of how God's grace has helped us through the hard times in our marriage and answering questions they have about honoring the Lord as a gospel-centered, Christ-reflecting married couple.

Benefits of Serving Together as a Married Couple

Serving together brings benefit not only to others but also to our own marriage. We have the privilege of seeing the hand of God in our spouse's life in fresh ways. We realize just how much our spouse contributes to the work of the Lord. That increases our gratitude for his grace in the one we love so much. We see how much we need our spouse and our spouse needs us. That mutual trust and honor in marriage reflects one of God's purposes for creating Adam and Eve and bonding them together as husband and wife. In this way, they more fully carried out the mission God had given his image-bearers than they could have done as isolated individuals.

A married couple that I am looking forward to getting to know in glory is Prisca (also known as Priscilla) and Aquila. They are mentioned repeatedly in the Bible (Acts 18:26; 1 Corinthians 16:19; 2 Timothy 4:19), but not with a lot of detail other than the fact that they always seemed to be involved in ministry *together*. Paul commended them this way in Romans 16:3, "Greet Prisca and Aquila, my fellow workers in Christ Jesus." Did you catch that? Paul referred to this married couple as "my fellow workers in Christ Jesus." Now wouldn't that be a wonderful way for any of us couples to be remembered?

One of our wedding gifts from long ago that has made a difference in our life as a married couple is a wall plaque reflecting these memorable words from British missionary C. T. Studd: "Only one life, 'twill soon be past. Only what's done for Christ will last." Yes. Let us not waste our marriages in the second half of our lives. Let us serve Christ together.

Questions

1. Sit down with your spouse and discuss gifts you see in each other that might be used to bless others in service.
2. Take time to work through the *who, where, what, when,* and *why* questions with your spouse.
3. Which *what ifs* strike a chord with you? What will help you and your spouse work through those together so they don't hinder you from serving?
4. What action steps could you and your spouse take in response to reading this chapter?

Chapter 10

Welcoming: Pursuing Purposeful Friendships

EVEN A CASUAL online search for the challenges and perils facing today's older generation reveals a plethora of articles focusing on the problem of isolation among seniors. Some of this isolation experienced by older people is understandable. Their days of interacting with coworkers in places of employment are behind them. Maybe they have moved to a retirement community or a new city to be closer to their children and grandchildren, leaving longtime friends behind. As they continue their journey into their elderly years, it is normal for their mobility to decrease. No longer is it easy to get out for social gatherings. And for those in their most senior years, the day comes when they realize they have outlived most of their old friends. Sociologists, psychologists, and medical personnel have documented that older people who are socially isolated have higher rates of depression and dementia and tend to die at a younger age than their more socially connected peers.

Why is there a connection between social isolation and a decline in the physical, mental, and emotional health of people in their senior years? What can Christians do to reverse this trend and prevent it in their own marriages, families, churches, and communities?

We Were Made for Relationship

One of the most encouraging themes throughout the Bible is the story of God wanting to be *with* us. He made human beings to be in relationship with him in ways that are not possible for any other creature. When Genesis 3:8 tells us that Adam and Eve heard "the LORD God walking in the garden in the cool of the day," the implication is that this wasn't the first time that happened. Apparently, God had come on other days to walk and talk with his image-bearers, Adam and Eve. God took the initiative to be *with* them, making Eden a sacred place—a sort of "temple" where God would come to meet with his people. How sad when Adam and Eve's sinful rebellion led to their expulsion from this temple-garden.

But God didn't abandon his commitment to be in relationship with his people. He promised that one day he would send a Serpent Crusher (Genesis 3:15) to undo the damage and heal the breach that sin had brought. In the intervening years, God told Moses and the Israelites to build a tabernacle, putting it in the middle of the camp because God wanted to be *with* his people.

Then that glorious day arrived when "the Word became flesh and dwelt among us" (John 1:14). God had come in the flesh in the person of Jesus Christ to be *with* us. Even after Jesus died, rose again, and ascended to heaven, he sent the Holy Spirit to come be *with* us (Acts 1:5). And what do we have to look forward to? When Christ returns, we will hear "a loud voice from the throne saying, 'Behold, the dwelling place of God is *with* man. He will dwell with them, and they will be his people, and God himself will be *with* them as their God'" (Revelation 21:3, emphases added). There is so much encouragement—so much power—in that little word *with*. God wants to be *with* us.

God made his image-bearers to be in relationship not only with him but also with one another. The Creator said, "It is not good that the man should be alone; I will make him a helper fit for him" (Genesis 2:18). The man needed a relational "completer," and God designed Eve to be Adam's wife and co-regent. When sin entered the human race on that dreadful day, the relationship between the Creator and his creations was not the only one damaged. The relationship between Adam and Eve, the first husband and wife, was also damaged. Adam blamed Eve for his own sin (Genesis 3:12), and God announced that Eve would struggle in her relationship with her husband from that day on (Genesis 3:16).

God could have abandoned his image-bearers, giving up any attempts to heal their relationship that was broken by their rebellion. He could have left the husband and wife in unrelenting division and distance. But he didn't. God pursued sinners. God pursued us, sending his own Son to pay the penalty for our sinful rebellion and heal broken relationships, both vertically with him and horizontally with one another.

So there is a reason deeper than the world understands why isolation has such a devastating impact on human beings—a *spiritual* reason. God made us to be in relationship with him and with one another, and it is only through the gospel that this spiritual disease of isolation can be healed. God's attention-grabbing commitment to pursue us, his astonishing motivation and the amazing price he paid to bring us back to himself is encapsulated in this one memorable sentence: "For God so loved the world, that he gave his only Son, that whoever believes in him should not perish but have eternal life" (John 3:16).

There are days in our Christian experience—hard days—when we might question, *Does Jesus really love me?* Where do we go to have our disturbed minds calmed and our unsettled hearts assured? We go not to our current circumstances; we go back to the cross. Hours before his death, Jesus assured his disciples, "Greater love has no one than this, that someone lay down his life for his friends" (John 15:13). Jesus calls us his *friends*! He died to transform his enemies (us!) into his friends (Romans 5:8). Now he calls us to reflect his love for us in our love for one another: "This is my commandment, that you love one another as I have loved you" (John 15:12).

Are the potential benefits of being healthier physically and happier mentally good motivations for us to pursue friendships in our seasoned years? Sure they are. But there is a more significant reason—a more foundational reason. God wants us to be in relationship with others to reflect *him*. That's a key reason he made us and why he redeemed us at such a cost. Friendships are not merely one of the options for us to consider for our own well-being in our second half of life. Friendships are to be intentionally pursued for God's glory and our good. So what friendships should a Christ-following couple pursue in the second half of life?

Pursuing Friendships with Those Ahead of Us

What friends do you—or could you—have who are further along life's path than you are? One day, we'll look around and realize we are the oldest person in the room in nearly every context. But for most of us, that day hasn't come yet. We know some precious older saints who have followed and served Christ longer than we have. What might pursuing a friendship with one (or a few) of them look like? What could be some benefits and blessings for you and for them?

When Gladine and I were in the early years of life's second half, we were hungry to have some godly older people in our lives. We reached out to a widow and a widower who were a generation older than we were. We invited them to be in our lives, and we asked if we could be in theirs. Over the course of their remaining years, they were wrapped into our life as a family. They became "Grandma Una Mae" and "Uncle Harold."

Our intergenerational relationships were not "projects" we were pursuing. These were our friends who became like family to us. We did life together. And now, decades later, we look back with fondness and gratitude for the impact each of those seasoned saints had on our lives. They told us life stories of blessings and challenges they had experienced. They pointed us to Christ and the joy we have in him through life's journey. We were blessed to have them as our friends, and in God's kindness, there must have been ways we blessed them too. When each of them died, we were humbled to be included as "family" at their memorial services.

What older person could you pursue a friendship with? It might be an older relative or an older person at your church who could benefit from having someone younger as a friend. How could you bless them? You might think of tasks you could do for them—offering to drive them to doctor appointments or do a chore that's physically demanding for them. But don't think *project*; think *friendship*. Ask them life questions. Listen to their stories. Share Scripture. Pray together. Cry together. Laugh together. You will be a blessing, and you will be blessed by pursuing a friendship with someone "ahead" of you on the path of life.

Pursuing Friendships with Those Alongside Us

Have you ever noticed how many "one anothers" there are in the Bible? The most well-known is "love one another" (found in John 13:34 and elsewhere), but these are also familiar:

- "encourage one another and build one another up" (1 Thessalonians 5:11)
- "bearing with one another" (Colossians 3:13)

- "forgiving each other" (Colossians 3:13; cf. Ephesians 4:32)
- "exhort one another" (Hebrews 3:13)
- "confess your sins to one another" (James 5:16)
- "pray for one another" (James 5:16)
- "bear one another's burdens" (Galatians 6:2)
- "stir up one another to love and good works" (Hebrews 10:24)

Please excuse me for asking an obvious question, but how are we supposed to fulfill these "one another" directives in the Bible if we live in isolation—without close Christian friends? God designed the Christian journey not to be a solo hike, but to be a band of spiritual brothers and sisters walking together and helping one another along the way. So what friendships do you currently have with those walking alongside you on the Christian journey? What friendships could you intentionally pursue, and how do you go about building those friendships?

Have you ever heard the saying, *We don't go to church, we are the church*? That's right, isn't it? Yet for many professing Christian couples, their nearly exclusive involvement in the life of the church is *going* to church. In other words, they walk into the weekly worship service right before the announced starting time, find a seat near someone they hardly know (or don't know at all), maybe join in the congregational singing, listen passively to the sermon, then make their exit as soon as the service is completed with no meaningful interaction with any other worship service attendees. Sadly, biblical friendships are not gained if this pattern continues.

What has to happen for couples in the second half of life to gain, enjoy, and benefit from friendships with their Christian peers? Change will require intentionality—to intentionally seize opportunities to get to know other believers on a deeper level than a friendly nod or quick handshake as they leave the weekly worship service. Why not begin by familiarizing your-self with relational opportunities your local church offers? Are there Sunday school classes, small group Bible studies, prayer gatherings, mission teams, or senior groups you could join? A few minutes spent exploring your church's website will prob-ably give you the information you need to find out where and when that group meets and whom to contact, if necessary, to make your first visit.

Is there something making you hesitate? Maybe you're more of an introvert and making that first visit feels intimi-dating. Is your spouse less of an introvert? Perhaps you could encourage one another to take this first step in building new friendships. That first step might be challenging, but if you give your involvement in that new setting some time to deepen, I think you will find the new friendships well worth the effort.

As you make new acquaintances, prayerfully and patiently move toward true friendships as the Lord graciously guides and encourages you. Make time to be together with people you are drawn to. Gladine and I have been impacted over the years by the life-shaping directive of Romans 12:13: "Seek to show hospitality." The word *hospitality* has to do with welcom-ing people into your life whom you really don't know that well to bless them. As we've seen, a literal translation of that com-mand could be "pursue hospitality." *Pursue* hospitality. That's more than just being willing to extend friendship to others. It denotes an intentional effort to make new friends. So let us *pursue* hospitality, intentionally inviting others into our lives for God's glory and their good.

Over time, our friendships deepen. We no longer spend our time together merely chitchatting about the weather, poli-tics, sports, and stories of how busy we are. We begin to move beyond our subtle attempts to outdo one another's "organ recitals" and "whine fests" as we report on our growing aches and pains. We begin to go deeper into one another's lives, helping one another deal with life's challenges and pointing one another to the hope we have in Christ.

More than twenty years ago, several men in our church committed to walk with me on this journey of following Jesus. Though some have moved away and others have joined our small band, a group of us have continued to meet nearly every Friday morning at a local restaurant. Not too surprisingly, we are all card-carrying senior citizens. We are affectionately known by others as "The Old Men for Christ," a moniker we gladly embrace.

Over our omelets and oatmeal, we talk about our lives, often on deep levels. There might be a short lapse into some comments on current political happenings or local news, but usually we are talking about our lives—how we're wrestling with a particular temptation, struggling to know how to best shepherd our wives through their own challenges, or grieving over a wayward child or grandchild. We listen to each other. We share encouraging Scriptures with one another. We challenge one another, reminded of these words of wisdom: "Iron sharpens iron, and one man sharpens another" (Proverbs 27:17) and "Faithful are the wounds of a friend" (Proverbs 27:6). We pray for one another. We love one another as a band of brothers.

While gender-specific friendships can have great, irreplaceable value, it is also helpful to have friends as a married couple. Other couples who are of similar age understand the challenges we all face in the second half of life. We can show compassion for one another. We can encourage one another with reminders of how we have seen the grace of God at work in one another's lives. We can stir hope, by God's grace, as we point one another to the trustworthiness of our heavenly Father.

Let us pursue friendships with fellow Christians who will be humbly courageous in helping us see our sin and lovingly gracious in pointing us to the power of the gospel. And may we be that kind of person for our friends.

Pursuing Friendships with Those Behind Us

Gladine and I were a bit caught off guard when a young, engaged couple in our church asked us if we would help prepare them for marriage. We thought they would logically be drawn to one of the younger staff couples in our church—a couple closer to their own age. When we got together for the first time as couples, we asked them why they wanted to meet with us. They told us it was *because* we were older! They *wanted* to learn from an older couple. I don't think this young couple is alone. I believe many younger individuals and couples in our churches and relational circles crave time with older couples. They want to hear the stories of our successes and failures. They want to hear stories of how we experienced the grace of God. They want to watch us relate to one another as husband and wife.

So are we willing to pursue friendships with people who are coming "behind" us—who are a generation or more younger than we are?

It is so easy for us to silo ourselves with our peers. The people in our age bracket tend to understand us. Their current life experiences are similar to ours. It's easier to stick with "our kind of people." But it's not God's way for us to cloister ourselves with our own generation. God's desire for us—his plan for us—is to be involved in the lives of those younger than we are for his glory and their good. "One generation shall commend your works to another, and shall declare your mighty acts" (Psalm 145:4). We are to "tell to the coming generation the glorious deeds of the LORD, and his might, and the wonders that he has done . . . that they should set their hope in God" (Psalm 78:4, 7). With God's commission on us as the older generation, let's be intentional in pursuing friendships with younger people. Let's start with our own family—our adult kids, grandchildren, and nieces and nephews.

Which younger people in your church could you invite into your lives as an older couple? Young people might feel awkward initiating the relationship, so we as the older generation can take the first step. An easy way to get started is to break out of the seniors-only group at your church. Are there some small groups or Bible studies that have younger people? Could you volunteer to help with the youth group in some capacity? Would your pastors recommend you to a young individual or couple for mentoring purposes? The possibilities are many. Let's pursue friendships with those coming behind us.

Pursuing Friendships with Sinners

Jesus's accusers meant it as slander when they called him "a friend of tax collectors and sinners!" (Luke 7:34). What sweet slander! We now sing in our worship times, "Jesus, what a friend of sinners." That's not slander to us. That's music to our ears because we know that we are the sinners whom Jesus has befriended by his astonishing grace.

How can we couples in this season of life reflect our Lord's heart by also befriending "sinners"? What friends do we have who still need God's saving grace? Maybe we need to look no further than our own extended family or our neighborhood. There are people around us who are still without Christ in their lives. How might we reach out to them, not as a "project" but as friends? How could we show them the love of Christ by our actions and the power of the gospel in our daily lives? Think of the possible response of showing these friends the treasure who is Christ: "In your hearts honor Christ the Lord as holy, always being prepared to make a defense to anyone who asks you for a reason for the hope that is in you; yet do it with gentleness and respect" (1 Peter 3:15). By God's sovereign grace, these currently nonbelieving friends might become our eternity friends. Wouldn't that be glorious?

May we find great joy during our seasoned years in the friendships we pursue with people of all ages. And may we bring joy to our friends as we reflect our Lord who has graciously called us his friends (John 15:15).

Questions

1. Ponder the truth that Jesus calls his followers his friends. What effect would it have on your life to carry this truth with you through your daily routine?

2. Take stock of the friendships you have as individuals and as a couple. Does each of you have friends? Do the two of you together have friends? Are all of your friends approximately the same age as you? Do you have friends who are older than you? Do you have friends who are younger than you? Where are the holes that you might be blessed by filling?

3. Pray and consider with your spouse how you could broaden your friendship base or deepen the friendships you already have.

Chapter 11

Accepting: Facing Physical Changes

IT USUALLY STARTS with a second look in a brightly lit mirror. *Wait! Is that a gray hair?* And we pluck it. Then we realize one day that our arms are no longer long enough to hold a document at a readable distance. So we get reading glasses. (By the way, it's called *presbyopia*—literally, "old person's eyes." Sorry. I just thought you would like to know that tidbit of medical knowledge.) Soon, we notice that we're getting up during the night to use the bathroom more frequently. We notice wrinkles. We have aches and pains that we don't remember feeling in the past. And as one year gives way to the next, we notice even more signs of aging. Our bodies are changing, and many of the changes are not encouraging.

Look at how the writer of Ecclesiastes, with all his masterful metaphors, describes aging:

> Don't let the excitement of youth cause you to forget your Creator. Honor him in your youth before you grow old and say, "Life is not pleasant anymore." Remember him before the light of the sun, moon, and stars is dim to your old eyes, and rain clouds continually darken your sky. Remember him before your

legs—the guards of your house—start to tremble; and before your shoulders—the strong men—stoop. Remember him before your teeth—your few remaining servants—stop grinding; and before your eyes— the women looking through the windows—see dimly. Remember him before the door to life's opportunities is closed and the sound of work fades. Now you rise at the first chirping of the birds, but then all their sounds will grow faint.

Remember him before you become fearful of falling and worry about danger in the streets; before your hair turns white like an almond tree in bloom, and you drag along without energy like a dying grasshopper, and the caperberry no longer inspires sexual desire. Remember him before you near the grave, your everlasting home, when the mourners will weep at your funeral. (Ecclesiastes 12:1–5 NLT)

How is the Christian supposed to prepare for and respond to these physical changes that come with the aging process? How is the Christian married couple supposed to serve one another when they see their spouse impacted by limiting and even debilitating physical changes? How can they apply the truths of God's Word to shape their responses to the physical changes that come with advancing years?

The Reality That We Are Gradually Wasting Away

When Paul wrote in Romans 8:18, "For I consider that the sufferings of this present time are not worth comparing with the glory that is to be revealed to us," what present sufferings was he referring to? It's clear in the context that he was not drawing attention to some specific hardship he was experiencing at the time he wrote this letter. He was writing about the reality of life in a fallen world. Life can be hard, and it seems to get harder in the second half of life. That seems especially evident when we take an honest assessment of our physical condition during our older years.

When I turned forty years old (forty, mind you), a fun-loving yet insightful eleven-year-old niece gave me a hand-drawn birthday card. On the front was a simple line drawing of a hill with a person on a sled going down the far side. Inside the card were these words in her adolescent handwriting that both amused and sobered me: *Uncle Larry, you are over the hill now, and you know what's at the bottom!* Even if that does seem to be a morbid thought for an eleven-year-old, it's true, isn't it? And in case you're wondering, yes, I still love my niece to this day.

Though I might no longer see forty as being "over the hill," it is reality that somewhere in our forties most of us crossed the halfway mark of our journey through life. From then on, we have fewer years ahead of us than we have behind us. And as we journey through our second half, we realize that we're going downhill—at least physically. Unless we suffer a sudden, unexpected medical calamity such as a stroke, heart attack, or serious accident, our physical decline will be gradual—like going down that hill my niece drew for me.

At first, our speed of decline seems relatively insignificant. There are those little things that we notice changing in our bodies. But in God's kindness, we're still almost as active as we were in our younger years. We have a friend who refers to this part of our second half of life as the "Go! Go!" years. We can still push ourselves to accomplish most of the physical tasks that we attempt.

But somewhere along life's journey, our downhill speed seems to accelerate. It gets harder and harder to do those tasks and accomplish those goals that we were used to doing without much effort in our younger years. We notice more and more physical losses. Our previously enjoyed youthful appearance and athleticism are becoming more of a memory than a present reality. Our eyesight and hearing change—but not for the better. Heavy objects that we previously carried without much effort in the past now give us pause: *Should I or shouldn't I? Maybe it would be better to ask someone younger to move it for me.* And what happened to my "gas tank"? Did it shrink somewhere along the way? More and more often, it seems that I run out of gas before I run out of day. Sexual relations with our spouse require more intentionality, and the hard-to-contain physical passion of our younger years is no longer a regular experience. Yes, the decline in our bodies is noticeable. Our friend calls these the "Slow Go" years.

If we live long enough, some of us will experience the "No Go" years. Our physical decline gradually gives way to a life of dependence on others to do daily tasks that we did for ourselves over most of our lives. Maybe you or your spouse have suffered a stroke or a heart attack, suddenly needing someone else to provide necessary assistance in moving, eating, bathing, dressing, and toileting. The physical losses of the "No Go" years can seem all consuming. These are only some of the physical present sufferings of living our second half of life in this fallen world.

How are we Christians supposed to think about these physical changes in our second half? How are we to respond? And how are we to come alongside our spouses in order to help them navigate the physical declines and losses they are also encountering?

We grow. First, we must grow in understanding and accepting the reality that the sin that entered the human race has had negative consequences—including bodily consequences—for all of us. What did God say to our ancestor Adam? "And the LORD God commanded the man, saying, 'You may surely eat of every tree of the garden, but of the tree of the knowledge of good and evil you shall not eat, for in the day that you eat of it *you shall surely die*'" (Genesis 2:16–17, emphasis added). But Adam *did* eat of that tree. He committed an act of treason against his good and gracious King, and what was the verdict? "For you are dust, and *to dust you shall return*" (Genesis 3:19, emphasis added). And as Paul summarized in Romans 5:12, "Just as sin came into the world through one man, and death through sin, and so death spread to all men because all sinned." Our physical decline that leads to death sobers us, reminding us of our place in the fallen human race and our personal need for Someone to rescue us from this plight.

We pray. We pray for God to forgive us for our sin—our part in the rebellion against him as our Creator and King—trusting in his complete forgiveness. The good news is "if you confess with your mouth that Jesus is Lord and believe in your heart that God raised him from the dead, you will be saved" (Romans 10:9). We pray for his help in living in this fallen world, including all the hardships we experience in this challenging season of life. "Do not cast me off in the time of old age; forsake me not when my strength is spent" (Psalm 71:9).

We thank God for the blessings of our older years. Yes, the blessings. "Wisdom is with the aged, and understanding in length of days" (Job 12:12). "Gray hair is a crown of glory; it is gained in a righteous life" (Proverbs 16:31). "The glory of young men is their strength, but the splendor of old men is their gray hair" (Proverbs 20:29). Rather than devaluing our older years, let us embrace them with gratitude for the blessings they bring.

We groan. There is no reason to deny the reality of our present sufferings and the pain they bring into our lives, including physical suffering. The Bible doesn't hide the fact that we Christians suffer in life. There is an honesty in the Bible that makes us lean in with agreement. We groan with our daily aches and pains. We groan over the deeper losses we experience in our second half of life.

But—and this is key—our groaning is not the despairing groan of a person who does not know Jesus, but the Christian's groaning of desire—of anticipation. Pause and ponder these insightful words of Romans 8:22–23: "For we know that the whole creation has been groaning together in the pains of childbirth until now. And not only the creation, but we ourselves, who have the firstfruits of the Spirit, groan inwardly as we wait eagerly for adoption as sons, *the redemption of our bodies*" (emphasis added).

Like a woman groaning with the pains of childbirth, our groaning is a response to pain, yes, but not the pain of hopeless despair. The woman in labor is groaning with anticipation of embracing her soon-to-be-born child. Our groaning as believers is like that. Ours is a groaning of anticipation as we look forward to the time of the promised return of Jesus, the lifting of the curse of Genesis 3, and the great physical resurrection when we receive our glorified, sinless, eternal, pain-free bodies. We know that what we suffer now is "not worth comparing with the glory that will be revealed in us" (Romans 8:18 NIV). The Holy Spirit "helps us in our weakness" (Romans 8:26), taking that Bible-informed knowledge of what God has promised for our eternal future and rooting it in our hearts, producing hope in the midst of our present suffering.

Evaluating Dominant Cultural Perspectives on Our Aging Bodies

Responses to the physical changes encountered in the second half of life vary from person to person and from couple to couple. Some people seem to be living in denial that the aging process will ever catch up to them. They dread the idea of experiencing physical decline, devoting loads of time, money, and energy in their attempt to keep the aging process at bay. Interestingly, other people just give up, adopting a melancholic demeanor that communicates, *What's the use? Why fight it?*

I'm going to die anyway. What's behind these polar responses to the physical changes that come over the years of our second half? Where do these perspectives come from? Though these perspectives on our bodies seem to be opposite, they do have something in common: both of them leave God and his Word out of the picture.

There are people who treat their bodies as if they don't matter. They neglect their bodies and abuse their bodies through physically damaging, life-dominating addictions like smoking, alcohol and drug abuse, lack of exercise, overeating, and constantly consuming unhealthy foods. Others neglect their bodies because they are racked by depression. And sadly, some professing Christians have naively adopted not a biblical theology of the body, but an ancient world philosophy that says, *The soul is what counts. The body doesn't matter all that much because it is temporal. When we die, we will be finally released from our bodies. Only our souls last into eternity.* This rationale for neglecting our bodies goes against God and his Word.

Much more prevalent in our culture, though, is the bent toward idolizing our bodies. Even Christian men and women can be sucked into the quest for the "fountain of youth." Businesses play on people's assumption that their worth is found in their appearance and that *as long as you have your health, you have everything.* Succumbing to their fears and desires, they spend astonishing amounts of money and time pursuing youthfulness—or at least the appearance of youthfulness—through cosmetic surgery, the latest diet, this year's clothing styles, gym memberships, and miracle supplements. What is missing from our culture's obsession with youth is an orientation toward God and what he has said about our bodies. The quest for eternal physical youth is founded on the belief that this life is all there is, so we must hang onto it at all costs. What is the biblical alternative?

Our Bodies Matter to God

The biblical view avoids both extremes. On the one hand, the Bible affirms that our bodies are important. God made the human body. Think about these verses from the opening pages of the Bible: "The Lord God formed the man of dust from the ground and breathed into his nostrils the breath of life, and the man became a living creature" (Genesis 2:7). "The rib that the Lord God had taken from the man he made into a woman" (v. 22). "God saw everything that he had made, and behold, it was very good" (1:31). It's helpful for us to remember that physical bodies were part of God's plan for his image-bearers right from the beginning.

Rather than thinking of our bodies as something of lesser importance than our spirits or as mere temporal vehicles for our souls to one day be discarded, the Bible paints a very different picture. Not only did God plan for the first people to have physical bodies, but he also has planned for his redeemed people to have physical bodies in eternity too. Many well-meaning-but-mistaken Christians assume that we "shed" our bodies at death in order to live for the rest of eternity in a body-free state. That is not what our heavenly Father has planned for us. He is planning to clothe us with new, glorified bodies upon the return of Jesus. First Corinthians 15:53 assures us, "This perishable body must put on the imperishable, and this mortal body must put on immortality."

Physical bodies mattered to God at the beginning, and our physical bodies will matter to God at the end. Even now, in this era between the garden of Eden and the garden of the new earth, God cares about our bodies. Paul is correcting wrong thinking when he writes in 1 Corinthians 6:13 that our bodies are for God and God is for our bodies. He concludes that teaching with, "Or do you not know that your body is a temple of the Holy Spirit within you, whom you have from God? You are not your own, for you were bought with a price. So glorify God in your body" (1 Corinthians 6:19–20).

Because Our Bodies Matter to God, They Matter to Us

Because it is clear in the Bible that God made our bodies, redeems our bodies, and will one day restore our bodies, our bodies must matter to us. We see our bodies as a gift from God that he wants us to steward for his glory, our good, and the blessing of others, including our spouses.

We steward our bodies as we continue our journey through the second half of life by caring for them with thoughtful intentionality. When we consider our eating and drinking habits, we do so to the glory of God (1 Corinthians 10:31). We get age-appropriate exercise as we are able to maintain as much mobility as we can in serving our spouses and others. We rest and sleep as an expression of our trust in our sovereign Father who never sleeps nor slumbers. We keep our doctor appointments and take medications as an expression that we accept the effects of living in a fallen world and God's provision of these means of caring for our bodies.

On the other hand, the Bible also teaches us that our current physical bodies are not ultimate. They are imperfect and temporary. When Paul writes about our future physical resurrection, he contrasts our current perishable bodies with the imperishable bodies we shall be given on that glorious day (1 Corinthians 15:42–43). Knowing that one day our current weak and temporary bodies will be replaced with powerful and eternal bodies, we resist the world's tendency to idolize our present bodies. With this biblical balance, we care for our bodies as gifts from God to be used for his glory and the good of others while not succumbing to the world's obsession with making the health and youthfulness of our bodies our life's priority.

We Devote Ourselves to Caring for Our Spouse in the Second Half of Life

Unless there is a significant age gap between us and our spouse, the reality is that our husband or wife is feeling the effects of the aging process alongside us. We vowed on our wedding day to love our spouse "in sickness and in health." That sacred promise takes on new depth as we journey into our older years. We feel our need for one another in fresh ways as we age.

There are those seemingly small ways we reflect Christ's love to our spouse: helping one another to remember to take our medications on time or assisting one another in climbing the stairs. Over time, the little ways we help become more significant: helping a spouse remember names and events when their memory is fading, caring for a debilitated spouse after surgery or a major health crisis, etc. Our spouse's body matters to God, and our spouse's body matters to us. Even when caring for a spouse's physical needs feels consuming, we recall our Savior who loved us and gave himself for us. Resting in his costly love, we show costly love to our spouse.

We Share Sexual Intimacy with Our Spouse in Our Second Half of Life

Advancing years and the decline of various physical abilities doesn't necessarily mean that an older couple can no longer provide sexual joy to one another. If the "fire" of earlier years has diminished to barely glowing embers, stir them! If the libido is lesser in these later years, showing each other sexual love might take more patience and planning, but it is worth it!

Take lots of time to talk. Your spouse might be feeling less attractive with an older body. Express your undying love, assuring your spouse of their attractiveness to you. Make tender touches a regular part of your interactions with one another. Hand holding, hugging, kissing, rubbing the back, and stroking the face or hair can all say, *I love you. I want you.* And even if sexual intimacy doesn't have the intensity of earlier years, it can still provide reassuring love. May you find joy in giving your spouse joy in this season of life.

As we journey through the physical challenges of increasing years, may we find fresh hope from this biblical blessing: "Now may the God of peace himself sanctify you completely, and may your whole spirit and soul *and body* be kept blameless at the coming of our Lord Jesus Christ" (1 Thessalonians 5:23, emphasis added).

Questions

1. How do you view the aging process? What are your biggest fears as you look ahead? Take some time to pray through them.

2. Consider your own view of your body. Do you lean toward one extreme view or the other? If so, how is this chapter's discussion of the biblical view of the body helpful?

3. What is one thing you could do—or stop doing—to make your sexual relationship more fulfilling for your spouse?

4. The difficulties of aging are often clearer in our minds than the benefits. Spend some time meditating on what the Bible says about old age: Job 12:12; Proverbs 16:31 and 20:29.

Chapter 12

Trusting: Dealing with Financial Changes

ONE OF THE most common concerns for couples in the second half of life is their financial security. For those in the preretirement years, the questions tend to be, *Will we have enough to retire when we want to? Are we going to have to work until we're old and decrepit?* Those who are already retired tend to ask, *What if we outlive our savings? We can't make it on Social Security alone! What's going to happen to us?*

There are many subpoints to these concerns—or do we call them worries?

- Look at the rising cost of health care! It's just getting worse! Do you know how much we pay for medications every month?
- What if we need major repairs on our house? That would make a huge dent in our budget.
- How are we going to pay off our debts? I can't believe how much we owe on our credit cards! I thought we would have our mortgage paid off by now.
- What if inflation takes off again? We're on a fixed income. We can't keep up with the rising costs of our groceries, gas, and car repairs!

- The market is so volatile! What if it crashes? All those years of sacrificing to save up for our retirement years could be wiped out in a day!
- Look, we don't want to end up being a burden to our kids. What are we supposed to do?

Facing Financial Concerns as a Couple

Most couples have intense conversations about finances now and then. Even though many couples in the second half of life have been married for decades, the debates over finances haven't necessarily diminished, let alone disappeared. In fact, approaching the transition to retirement can lead to some of the most stressful discussions over finances that many couples have ever had. The uncertainty of what lies ahead can prompt strain between the husband and wife as they struggle to come to a position of unity on issues of spending, saving, and giving, especially once the faucet to their previous primary source of income has been shut off. How can a Christian couple in this season of life come to a position of peaceful, and even joyful, unity?

Each person trying to forcibly win their spouse over to their viewpoint on finances rarely bears good fruit. Nobody enjoys being pushed into a position that they don't prefer. Trying to find a happy medium between their two viewpoints might work in some areas of disagreement, but it won't work for every situation. What could be a better way forward? Consider these steps:

Pray together, humbly acknowledging to the Lord the differences you are dealing with and your need for his unifying grace and wisdom. Once again, take hope in God's promise that he gives wisdom "generously to all without reproach" to those who ask (James 1:5). Remember his promise to be with you and to guide you when you are unsure of the way ahead. "I will lead the blind in a way that they do not know, in paths that they have not known I will guide them. I will turn the darkness before them into light, the rough places into level ground. These are the things I do, and I do not forsake them" (Isaiah 42:16).

Study God's Word together on the subjects of money, worry, trust, contentment, and generosity, taking notes on key lessons you want to apply to your own hearts and decisions. Not sure where to start? Take time to thoughtfully read through and discuss Bible passages such as Matthew 6:19–34, Luke 12:13– 31, 1 Timothy 6:17–19, Philippians 4:11–13, 2 Corinthians 8 and 9, Hebrews 13:5–6, and various Proverbs such as 15:16 and 30:8–9.

Humbly seek counsel from trusted, godly sources. Does your church offer classes or counseling for those who want to learn more about the Bible's teaching on financial issues? Ask your pastors for advice on books you could read or online videos you could watch that clearly teach a biblical perspective on money-related issues. Is there a financial planner you could meet with who not only understands the financial market but who also embraces God's teaching on our money and resources? "In an abundance of counselors there is safety" (Proverbs 11:14).

Process together what you are learning about viewing your finances from God's perspective and handling them in a way that honors him. Talk to each other. Listen to one another. How are each of you seeing your views of financial issues and your handling of your resources being shaped by God's Word? Are you finding common ground as you each release your grip on your own financial agenda and together take up God's?

Whose Money Is It, Anyway?

What would you estimate your net worth to be? For some of you, you don't even need a calculator! You could figure that out by using your fingers, or at least it feels that way. The bottom line for you is, shall we say, on the modest side. For others, answering that question might take some time. You might even be thinking, *I would need to check with my accountant or my broker to come up with the answer.* Either way, whether your answer is a rather small number or a rather large number, I have the same question: what percentage of your assets does God own?

If you answered, "God owns 100 percent of my resources," how does that conviction impact your daily life and financial decisions? If God owns it all, then you are no longer the ultimate *owner*, are you? You are more of a manager of *his* resources. How does that realization shape your view of "your" finances? How does that influence your decisions when it comes to financial matters? No longer do you have a feeling of entitlement—of deserving—but an attitude of responsibility. If all this money and all these resources ultimately belong to God, and if he has placed them under your care for this season of your lives, then you feel a need to be paying attention to his values and his purposes for these material assets, don't you? You want to be faithful stewards of his resources that he is entrusting to you.

Understanding Our Role as Stewards of God's Money

Growing a stewardship mindset about finances takes time and intentionality. Our natural inclination is to assume that the money and other resources under our care belong to us. Our default way of thinking is, *Hey, I worked hard for these resources. I earned them. They're mine.* So how might God's Word shape and transform our thinking from an *ownership* mindset to a *stewardship* mindset? Consider the following:

We can recall where our money and other possessions came from. In 1 Corinthians 4:7, Paul asks, "What do you have that you did not receive?" Consider King David's prayer in 1 Chronicles 29:11–13:

"Yours, O LORD, is the greatness and the power and the glory and the victory and the majesty, for all that is in the heavens and in the earth is yours. Yours is the kingdom, O LORD, and you are exalted as head above all. Both riches and honor come from you, and you rule over all. In your hand are power and might, and in your hand it is to make great and to give strength to all. And now we thank you, our God, and praise your glorious name."

We can learn from God's Word the purposes he has in entrusting us with his resources. He wants us to meet the daily needs of our family. "But if anyone does not provide for his relatives, and especially for members of his household, he has denied the faith and is worse than an unbeliever" (1 Timothy 5:8). God gives us resources so we can fulfill our financial obligations. He wants us to pay our taxes (Romans 13:6) and our creditors (Romans 13:7). The Lord directs us to use the resources he has put under our care to bless those who are in need: "But if anyone has the world's goods and sees his brother in need, yet closes his heart against him, how does God's love abide in him?" (1 John 3:17). God has given us financial resources so we can help fund the spread of the gospel. When the church at Philippi sent money to Paul, he described the gifts they sent as "a fragrant offering, a sacrifice acceptable and pleasing to God" (Philippians 4:18).

We are reminded in the Bible that, as managers of God's gifts, we will one day give an account for how we used his resources. "It is required of stewards that they be found faithful" (1 Corinthians 4:2). Remembering that responsibility of rightly using God's resources should lead us to use his money purposefully, and not assume that whatever he has placed in our hands can be carelessly spent on our own pleasures and pursuits.

Growing in Faithfulness as Stewards of God's Money

If you and your spouse have not yet developed the habit of regularly tracking where your money is going, now would be a great day to start. This will require some method of bookkeeping. Is one of you stronger in keeping track of details than the other? It might be wise for that person to be responsible for tracking your monthly expenditures.

If you don't already have a system, spend some time doing an online search for a budgeting app that would suit your situation and comfort level. Read reviews. Ask your friends for advice. If a system is too complicated, it is probable that you will soon abandon it. So pick one you can learn and use. Then start entering the pertinent data regarding your expenditures each month. After several months, sit down as husband and wife and evaluate. Are there some expenses that seem out of line, where you are spending too much in a particular area? With humility and grace toward each other, discuss reasonable ways to adjust the amount you have been spending for that category.

After you have had some months to track your expenditures, gaining a realistic picture of what it actually costs you to live month by month, block out some time as a couple to pray for God's wisdom and unity and begin to lay out monthly and annual budgets. As you choose the categories you are going to put into your budget, why not start with your giving to your local church and other worthy ministries? Should you add another line item for upcoming major expenses? Cars wear out. So do appliances, carpets, roofs, etc. By setting aside some money month by month, when you incur that major expense, you have the money available and are less likely to make that large purchase using credit with its accompanying high interest rate.

Using your budget as a guide, continue to track your expenditures, evaluating afresh each new year. Maybe you need to pare some expenses. Or you might decide that you need to increase how much you want to spend in some categories in order to be more generous givers to kingdom work or ministries of mercy. Maybe you will decide to bless one another by budgeting more money for a special anniversary getaway, for example. Our heavenly Father is not a scrooge! He "richly provides us with everything to enjoy" (1 Timothy 6:17).

You might be in a financial situation where you need to give some attention to debt. While some older couples have been able to gradually move to a position of being debt free, others still feel burdened with a mortgage, car payments, and outstanding credit card balances. How extensive is your debt? Is it manageable with your current income stream? Even if it is, might you grow in your stewardship of the money God has entrusted to you by reducing or even eliminating your indebtedness? The high interest rates on credit cards can be especially troublesome. As a couple, how could you discipline yourselves to pay off your balance each month with no interest charged? That would be a very good financial goal.

Is the debt load you are carrying especially heavy? Do you find yourself moaning an *amen* to the proverb that says "The borrower is the slave of the lender" (Proverbs 22:7)? If you are not yet retired, could you continue working longer than you had hoped, even on a part-time basis, in order to make headway on debt reduction? Are there some more serious steps you could take to get your financial footing? Move to more affordable housing? Sell some of your unnecessary possessions to get some cash to put toward your debt? Should you look for more affordable transportation? It might be time to seek the advice of a godly trusted financial advisor or counselor to work with you on a healthy financial plan. Above all, pray and ask for God's gracious provision. "Give us this day our daily bread" (Matthew 6:11).

Moving from Anxiety to Contentment with Our Finances

Financial worries are not new to the human race. In the first century, Jesus (in Matthew 6) and Paul (in Philippians 4:10–13

141

and 1 Timothy 6:8) addressed anxious people about their financial worries, seeking to help them let go of their anxieties and embrace contentment. Paul said that he *learned* contentment. His personal testimony was, "I have learned in whatever situation I am to be content. I know how to be brought low, and I know how to abound. In any and every circumstance, I have learned the secret of facing plenty and hunger, abundance and need. I can do all things through him who strengthens me" (Philippians 4:11–13).

If contentment can be learned, what do we read in God's Word that will help us make the journey from anxiety to contentment with our finances? Consider the following:

Money and the things that money buys don't ultimately satisfy the longings of our souls. The Preacher in Ecclesiastes 5:10 confesses after living a life of pursuing riches, "He who loves money will not be satisfied with money, nor he who loves wealth with his income; this also is vanity." Money and things were never designed to bring us a sense of security or significance. Only God himself can bring ultimate, lasting satisfaction in our souls. "He satisfies the longing soul, and the hungry soul he fills with good things" (Psalm 107:9; also see Psalm 16:11, John 4:13–14 and 6:35).

Money and the things that money buys don't last. In Matthew 6:19, Jesus says, "Do not lay up for yourselves treasures on earth, where moth and rust destroy and where thieves break in and steal." So what's the alternative? "Lay up for yourselves treasures in heaven, where neither moth nor rust destroys and where thieves do not break in and steal" (Matthew 6:20). Can't we older folks testify that we have personally witnessed the observation of Proverbs 23:4–5? "Do not toil to acquire wealth; be discerning enough to desist. When your eyes light on it, it is gone, for suddenly it sprouts wings, flying like an eagle toward heaven." It's true, isn't it? Why try to find security in that which will not last?

Money and the things that money buys don't count for eternity. In Luke 12:13–21 we have the record of a gripping parable that Jesus told. The story centers on a man who kept accumulating wealth for himself—more and more wealth, assuming that his stockpile of riches would guarantee him a luxurious retirement. This man assures himself, "You have ample goods laid up for many years; relax, eat, drink, be merry" (v. 19). Sounds kind of nice, doesn't it? That is, until you hear what God says to that man: "Fool! This night your soul is required of you, and the things you have prepared, whose will they be?" (v. 20). Wow! And what is Jesus's point in telling that parable? "So is the one who lays up treasure for himself and is not rich toward God" (v. 21). If we have been looking at our accumulated resources as if they will give us security, we need to be sobered by Jesus's reminder that money is not a reliable place to rest our hope.

As we see from God's Word that our wealth—whether great or small—is not worthy of our trust, and as we see that God himself *is* worthy, our anxiety begins to melt. So we look at our financial assets as temporary tools that we stewards can use for God's glory and his purposes. Our security comes not from the *gifts* he gives us, but from himself as the *Giver*.

Becoming More Generous with Our Money and Resources in This Season of Life

It is easy for us to assure ourselves that we would be more generous if we just had more money. But if we are not generous with what we have currently, why would we become more generous if we had more money in our accounts? Jesus highlighted the generosity of the widow who placed her two small coins in the offering box when he noted, "She out of her poverty put in all she had to live on" (Luke 21:4). Those with smaller portfolios can be quite generous when we see things the way Jesus does.

What would motivate a Christian couple to be generous with their resources? The secret is not found in looking *outward* at all the needs, then feeling guilted into doing one's duty in showing compassion. The secret is not found by looking *inward* at how being generous will make you feel good about yourself. No, the secret to being generous comes from looking *upward*, standing in astonishment at God's amazing grace in Christ. As Paul was encouraging the Corinthian believers to be generous, he drew their attention to the Lord Jesus: "For you know the grace of our Lord Jesus Christ, that though he was rich, yet for your sake he became poor, so that you by his poverty might become rich" (2 Corinthians 8:9).

God is the source of our joy, the security of our souls, and the supplier of our generosity. "Thanks be to God for his inexpressible gift!" (2 Corinthians 9:15).

Questions

1. What worries do you have about money? Which of the biblical reassurances in this chapter speak to your worries? Discuss with your spouse which of the practical suggestions on pages 136–37 you want to act on first.
2. With your spouse, reread the verses on money given in this chapter (Matthew 6:19–34; Luke 12:13–31; 1 Timothy 6:17–19; Philippians 4:11–13; 2 Corinthians 8 and 9; Hebrews 13:5–6; Proverbs 15:16, 30:8–9). Pray together and discuss what changes, if any, you need to make in the way you are viewing and handling your money.
3. How does acknowledging God as the owner and yourselves as the stewards of everything you have change your perspective on the money issues surrounding the second half of life?
4. Where do you struggle with discontentment? Ask God to help you learn contentment in this area.

Chapter 13

Finishing Well: Preparing for the End of Life

WHEN OUR CHILDREN were young, four or five times each year we would make the eight-hour road trip from Indiana to see our parents in Pennsylvania. We loved being with them, staying as long as we were able on most visits. That often meant a late-afternoon departure, with the return trip extending into the night hours, arriving back in Indiana well after the kids' usual bedtime. There was a particular place near the end of our journey where I would always wake up the kids by saying, "Time to get your shoes on! We're almost home!"

There comes a time in our second half of life when we realize we are nearing "home." It's time to get our shoes on! What does that involve? How do we prepare for the end of our life's earthly journey? How do we prepare our spouse and our family for our departure? Few of us have thought through the answers to those questions with much thoroughness. Even fewer of us have actually recorded in writing our end-of-life plans and shared them with our family members.

Unless Jesus comes back during our lifetime, we are all going to die. Every one of us. No exceptions. The Word of God is clear: "It is appointed for man to die once" (Hebrews 9:27). And as painful as it is to ponder, one of us in the marriage will experience the loss of our spouse. About 30 percent of people over the age of 65 are widowed, with most of those being women. By the age of 75, about 58 percent of women are widowed, as are 28 percent of men.[8] Knowing that every one of us is going to die, yet not knowing when that day will be, should move us to overcome our discomfort in talking about our upcoming death. Accepting the reality of our own death should move us to prepare for that time so that we might finish our journey well.

How do we do that? What are key aspects of preparing for the end of our lives? Begin by joining with your spouse in prayer, asking for the Lord's guidance as you prepare to end well on your journey together. "Trust in the LORD with all your heart, and do not lean on your own understanding. In all your ways acknowledge him, and he will make straight your paths" (Proverbs 3:5–6). Continuing to seek the Lord in prayer, make all the necessary preparations for the day when you will meet him—both the practical preparations and the personal and relational preparations. Leaning on God's wisdom and care, begin to organize for the end of your journey and beyond.

To help your family during your years of decline and after your death, consider preparing the following tangible documents, ideally having both printed and electronic versions organized and saved in safe locations, with all the appropriate persons (spouse, executor, alternative executor) knowing how to access them.

Preparing Your Personal Records

- What personal records will your survivors need to have available when you die? Here are some documents—or copies, if necessary—to gather: birth certificate, marriage license, divorce records, military records including veteran benefits, copies of driver's license, and Social Security card. Is there a record of both your father's and your mother's legal names at birth and birthplaces (needed for death certificate)? Include a list of each of your children, grandchildren, and great-grandchildren with up-to-date addresses for each.

- Is there some information about your home that survivors should be aware of? Security codes? Hidden house key? The location of a fireproof lockbox? The combination to a safe?
- Are there keepsake family letters, photos, or records that you hope stay in the family after you are gone? These could be included in the files to be given to your survivors.

Preparing Your Legal Documents

- It would be wise to have an initial meeting with an attorney to get advice on what documents would be helpful for your end-of-life concerns, as well as handling your estate. If possible, choosing an estate-planning attorney would be advisable—especially an attorney who is younger and likely to outlive you!
- Do you have a last will and testament? If so, when was the last time it was reviewed? Does it need to be updated? If you don't have a will, now is the time to work on that document.
- Ask your legal advisor if you should consider a revocable living trust.
- Who will have power of attorney over your financial and medical affairs in the event of your being incapacitated? Make sure you have done the necessary paperwork so that your affairs are handled properly.
- Do you have a living will to give direction to your spouse and family in making decisions about your

health care if you are unable to direct those decisions yourself?

- Is the deed for your home accessible? Your vehicle registrations?

Preparing Your Financial Documents

- As a couple, schedule a meeting with your financial planner and/or accountant. Ask for advice on end-of-life financial concerns to lessen the likelihood of missing important steps in preparing documents and information needed for those caring for your finances upon your incapacitation or death.
- Does your spouse or other close family member know how to access your financial documents? Do they know your passwords—or where to find them?
- Do they know how to access your bank accounts? Your investment information? Social Security benefits? Do they know how to find information on your credit cards and bills that are still outstanding upon your death?
- Are your insurance policies accessible? Any life insurance policies would be especially needed upon your death.
- Do you have mortgage and other real estate documents gathered and accessible?
- Having your tax returns from the last several years available for your surviving spouse or family member could be a time-saver.

Preparing Your Medical Records

- Keeping a record of chronic illnesses, especially if these might be hereditary, could be useful for your biological heirs.

- Keeping recent medical records will be helpful for the person handling your finances at the end of your life to discern what bills are paid and which, if any, are not.
- Health insurance records and agent contact information might be useful.
- A list of hospitals, doctors, and other health care providers is information that might be needed by those handling your estate.

Preparing Your Funeral and Burial Plans

- Choose a trusted funeral home, seeking advice for preplanning your and your spouse's funerals. Funeral home advisors have processes and procedures that will aid you in not forgetting helpful details in planning.
- Choosing a casket, vault, or cremation services, as well as other funeral services ahead of time, will take that burden off your surviving spouse and family members. Would it be helpful to prepay for upcoming funeral expenses? Alternatively, money could be set aside in a special fund among your own assets to cover your funeral costs.
- Purchasing a cemetery lot and headstone for the two of you while you are living means that your survivors will not have to do that upon your death. It would be a blessing for your family not to have to care for this detail in the days immediately after your passing.
- What are some of your preferences for your funeral? What pastor(s) would you like to preside, if they are available? Are there certain people you would like to participate in the service by reading a Scripture passage, giving a testimony, telling a

story, singing a hymn, or being a pallbearer? Do you have some favorite hymns or songs you would like played or sung congregationally?

- Gathering some of your personal history and some favorite photos might be helpful for whomever gives a eulogy at the service.
- Would you consider writing out the story of your salvation and spiritual journey in a concise form? This could be read in a way that honors your Savior and points those at your funeral to the One who is or could be their eternal hope as well.
- Some people assemble a list of names and contact information for extended family members, church contacts, friends, former coworkers, and neighbors to be informed of their passing and any pertinent funeral plans.

Doing the work of preparing, organizing, storing, and discussing these various tangible documents can be a wonderful way to show loving care to your surviving spouse and family members as you prepare for the end of your life, whenever that comes in the Lord's providential timing.

But there are nontangible ways you can prepare for the end of your earthly journey as well.

Preparing Your Own Heart

Facing your own death can bring a measure of anxiety, or even dread. Though we know there will be the inexpressible joy of seeing our Lord as well as believing loved ones who have preceded us in death, there's something about death that doesn't feel right.

That check in our souls when we think about our own upcoming deaths is understandable. We know that death has come because sin invaded and infected the whole human race.

If it were not for sin, there would be no death. We wouldn't die. But sin *is* here. Its ugly effects are evident in each of us and in the world around us. Death isn't natural in the grand scheme of eternity. That's why death is called an enemy—"the last enemy" to be killed (1 Corinthians 15:26) when Christ returns, completing his mission of living, dying, and rising again to rescue us from our sin and its consequences.

Facing our sure, upcoming death can understandably bring a measure of fear. What will it be like to die? How do we prepare our own hearts for death? Here are a few encouragements:

Cry out to God in prayer, asking for his help in overcoming your fear of dying. If you are not sure what to say to him, lean into the prayers of Psalm 71, making them the cry of your own heart. "Do not cast me off in the time of old age; forsake me not when my strength is spent" (v. 9). "In your righteousness deliver me and rescue me; incline your ear to me, and save me!" (v. 2).

Remind yourself that God has a sovereignly planned time for your death. You will die neither a day too early nor a day too late. "Your eyes saw my unformed substance; in your book were written, every one of them, the days that were formed for me, when as yet there was none of them" (Psalm 139:16).

Preach the gospel to yourself, recalling that you have no need to dread suffering God's judgment when you die. If you have placed your faith in Jesus Christ, there is no condemnation awaiting you. None. Jesus absorbed all of the condemnation you deserve when he died in your place on the cross. "There is therefore now no condemnation for those who are in Christ Jesus" (Romans 8:1).

Rest your weary soul in the assurance of God's presence, even as you pass through death's door. May the reality of the well-tested Psalm 23 bring comfort to you even as it has to millions of believers who have preceded you: "Even though I walk through the valley of the shadow of death, I will fear no evil, for you are with me; your rod and your staff, they comfort me" (v. 4). It's true. Not even death itself "will be able to separate us from the love of God in Christ Jesus our Lord" (Romans 8:39).

Thank God in a prayer of grateful worship. "You guide me with your counsel, and afterward you will receive me to glory. Whom have I in heaven but you? And there is nothing on earth that I desire besides you. My flesh and my heart may fail, but God is the strength of my heart and my portion forever" (Psalm 73:24–26).

Preparing Your Spouse's Heart

As hard as dying can be, the anguish of loss for the surviving spouse can be even deeper and is certainly longer. There's so much pain in having to say goodbye to your closest friend, your lover, the spouse to whom you promised your covenant love "till death do us part." The ache in the surviving spouse's heart is beyond words.

Assuming that you will be the first to die, how do you prepare your spouse's heart to outlive you? What can you say? What can you do? Consider these thoughts:

Express your love through your words. Tenderly look into your spouse's eyes and say those precious words: "I love you so much!"

Express your love through your actions. As you prepare your spouse for your upcoming departure, assure them of your love through hugs, kisses, and sensitive touches. Are there other tangible ways you could show your loving care for them as you think about your spouse living without you? Are there tasks you always took care of? If you are still able, why not take the time to show your spouse how to care for your financial obligations or how to cook some basic healthy meals or how to mow the lawn? The need will vary from couple to couple, but what is it you know how to do that your spouse doesn't? Could you either provide instruction so that your surviving spouse knows how to do that task or, alternatively, make arrangements for another family member or paid service to do that task when you're gone? Making these preparations for your spouse could ease their mind now and lighten their load in the future.

Express your gratitude. Saying thank you regularly for the daily things your spouse does for you is a wonderful way to reflect the grace of God in your marriage. But as you anticipate your death, consider expressing gratitude on a deeper level. What comes to my mind is something like, *Sweetheart, thank you for walking with me through life's journey. I'm so glad the Lord brought us together. There's no one else I would rather have had beside me all these years. You have been such an amazing blessing to me. Thank you.* Would you like to put an expression of your loving gratitude in writing that your spouse can reflect on again after you are gone? That might become a very precious blessing for your surviving spouse for years after you are gone.

Express grace-bathed sorrow for ways you could have loved your spouse better. Express with humble sincerity, "I am so sorry for not loving you as well as you have deserved over our years together. Will you forgive me?" When forgiveness is offered, show loving thankfulness. If your spouse similarly asks your forgiveness, grant it fully and freely.

Express praise, letting your spouse know how much you value them. What evidences of God's grace have you seen most clearly in your spouse? What Christ-reflecting attributes have you appreciated in your spouse over the years? Have you praised your spouse lately? Now is the time. As the time to say goodbye draws closer, wouldn't it be comforting for your spouse to hear reassuring words of appreciation such as "Many women have done excellently, but you surpass them all" (Proverbs 31:29)?

Express assurance of God's undying, unending, loving presence. Your spouse is probably grieving that they are able to walk you to the door of heaven but not able to walk you through.

They will have to say goodbye on this side, and that realization can be steeped in loving grief. Assure your spouse that you understand their grief, but share the comforting truth that you will not be walking through the door of death alone. Escorting you into heaven will be your ever-present Lord, who promised, "I will never leave you nor forsake you" (Hebrews 13:5). Take your spouse's hand and say, "It is okay. He will hold me fast."

Preparing Your Family's Hearts

Similar to your care for your spouse, you will want to prepare your surviving family for your upcoming death, as the Lord enables you. As you are able to, connect personally with your children and grandchildren, being intentional in moving beyond the chitchat of life or the reports of your current physical condition. As with your spouse, speak words of love, gratitude, confession, forgiveness, and praise. As the Lord guides you, perhaps write personal letters to your individual family members—even those with whom your relationship has been distant—expressing your love and appreciation. A written (or video) record of your love for each one personally might be treasured for years to come.

Many people leave a will that pertains to the physical resources they will leave behind, and that is appropriate. But what if you also left a "spiritual will" for your family? Psalm 71:18 provides a model prayer for your family's spiritual well-being: "So even to old age and gray hairs, O God, do not forsake me, until I proclaim your might to another generation, your power to all those to come."

Leaving a written spiritual will for your family might be a powerful way to proclaim the glories of God to the coming generation. In your own words, express your love and gratitude for them. Tell them of your spiritual journey—how the Lord brought you to saving grace, how you have seen his hand on your life over the years, and how you are trusting him in these latter steps of your earthly journey. Relate to your family how much you are looking forward to seeing your Savior. Intersperse Bible verses that are precious to you and, Lord willing, encouraging to your family.

A key element in a spiritual will is a clear, loving expression of your desire that your family members also put their faith in Christ alone, treasuring him and living for him over the course of their own journeys. Consider ending your spiritual will by writing a blessing over your family. As an example, consider the Aaronic blessing of Numbers 6:24–26: "The LORD bless you and keep you; the LORD make his face to shine upon you and be gracious to you; the LORD lift up his countenance upon you and give you peace"—and as one of my co-pastors always adds at the end, "in Christ."

Another consideration is giving a loving appeal to your children and grandchildren that they look after your spouse— their parent or grandparent—after you are gone. The Bible is clear that families are to care for their widows. First Timothy 5:3–4 reminds us, "Honor widows who are truly widows. But if a widow has children or grandchildren, let them first learn to show godliness to their own household and to make some return to their parents, for this is pleasing in the sight of God."

Glorifying God in Your Death

Toward the end of his gospel, John records a summary of a conversation the resurrected Jesus had with Peter about his future death. In relating this story, John adds this parenthetical statement: "This he said to show by what kind of death he was to glorify God" (John 21:19). I'm not sure I understand fully all that this implies, but I'm captivated by the idea that we can glorify God in our death. How can we do that? How do you draw your family's attention to God's glory—the weight and overwhelming beauty of his greatness and grace—in how you face death? We can do this by doing the following:

- Look at the *past* with gratitude for God's faithful love in your life. "The steadfast love of the LORD never ceases; his mercies never come to an end; they are new every morning; great is your faithfulness" (Lamentations 3:22–23).
- Look at the *present* with faith in God's unfailing care. "Even to your old age I am he, and to gray hairs I will carry you" (Isaiah 46:4).
- Look at the *future* with sure hope in soon seeing God's face—the very "heaven of heaven." "No longer will there be anything accursed, but the throne of God and of the Lamb will be in it, and his servants will worship him. They will see his face" (Revelation 22:3–4).

We're almost home. Time to get your shoes on!

Questions

1. Look over the list of papers and documents you should have in order and accessible to those who survive you. What have you already taken care of? What remains to be taken care of? Identify one item to tackle first. Consider enlisting someone to hold you (and your spouse) accountable for completing this task.

2. How do you feel as you consider your own death? Has the way you feel about death changed over the years? How do you feel as you consider the death of your spouse? With your spouse, read the verses on pages 151–52. Then pray together, reminding yourself of God's promises to his precious children and asking him to strengthen your trust in him.

3. What does a death that glorifies God look like?

Conclusion

"Well Done"

WITH TEARS ON your cheeks and a smile on your face, the day will come when one of you walks your spouse to heaven's gate, knowing that your earthly journey together has ended, even as heaven awaits. When you reflect on the beginning of your journey together in marriage, were your wedding vows similar to the ones we made on that warm June day decades ago? "I, Larry, take you, Gladine, to be my wedded wife, to have and to hold, from this day forward, for better, for worse, for richer, for poorer, in sickness or in health, to love and to cherish till death do us part."

On your wedding day, you probably thought the "till death do us part" commitment was more of a sweet sentiment. You probably didn't foresee the day it would actually come to be. But here you are in the second half of life. For many seasoned couples, you know that your day of parting is closer than your wedding day. Eventually, it will be your turn to walk through heaven's gate.

What Will You Say?

Don't we long to be able to repeat the words of Paul as he faced his impending death? "I have fought the good fight, I have finished the race, I have kept the faith. Henceforth there is laid up for me the crown of righteousness, which the Lord, the righteous judge, will award to me on that day, and

not only to me but also to all who have loved his appearing"
(2 Timothy 4:7–8).

What Will You See?

While many Christians first think of seeing their spouse and
other family members who preceded them to heaven—and
so they shall—seeing our Lord is what will first captivate us
upon our arrival in eternity. From the first chapter of the Bible
to the last, the breathtaking story is that God wants us to be
with him—and he with us. Ponder the promise of Revelation
21:3: "Behold, the dwelling place of God is with man. He will
dwell with them, and they will be his people, and God himself
will be with them as their God." Seeing his face will make the
struggles of this life fade away. "For I consider that the sufferings of this present time are not worth comparing with the
glory that is to be revealed to us" (Romans 8:18).

What Will You Hear?

I have little doubt that nearly every believer longs to hear the
most blessed words any person could ever be told. Can you
imagine the joy and reassurance of hearing from the lips of our
gracious, glorified Savior, "Well done, good and faithful servant. . . . Enter into the joy of your master" (Matthew 25:21)?
Now what if (and I know this is my imagination) the Savior
added, "You were so faithful in loving my daughter (your
wife)/my son (your husband)! In your marriage, you two were
a beautiful reflection of the greatest love story ever—my love
for my redeemed bride, the church. Thank you!" Doesn't just
thinking about that inspire us to finish our journey together as
husband and wife with Christ-reflecting love and grace?

What Will You Experience?

As we, the redeemed, come to the heavenly Zion (Hebrews
12:22), we will experience the fulfillment of this ancient

promise of God to Israel, "The ransomed of the LORD shall return and come to Zion with singing; everlasting joy shall be upon their heads; they shall obtain gladness and joy, and sorrow and sighing shall flee away" (Isaiah 51:11).

And that will make our years together in marriage a well-spent journey. Amen.

Notes

Chapter 1

1. Larry E. McCall, *Loving Your Wife as Christ Loves the Church* (BMH Books, 2009), 9.

Chapter 3

2. "Median Age at First Marriage: 1890 to Present," United States Census Bureau, U.S. Department of Commerce, 2023, https://www.census.gov/content/dam/Census/library/visualizations/time-series/demo/families-and-households/ms-2.pdf.

Chapter 4

3. Susan L. Brown and I-Fen Lin, "The Graying of Divorce: A Half Century of Change," OUP Academic, April 6, 2022, https://academic.oup.com/psychsocgerontology/article/77/9/1710/6564346.

4. Larry E. McCall, *Grandparenting with Grace: Living the Gospel with the Next Generation* (New Growth Press, 2019), 70.

Chapter 6

5. See Area Agency on Aging, https://areaagencyonaging.org/.

Chapter 7

6. "Caregiver Statistics: Demographics," Family Caregiver Alliance, 2016, https://www.caregiver.org/resource/caregiver-statistics-demographics/.

7. Adapted from Larry E. McCall, *Grandparenting with Grace: Living the Gospel with the Next Generation* (New Growth Press, 2019).

8. Benjamin Gurrentz and Yeris Mayol-Garcia, "Marriage, Divorce, Widowhood Remain Prevalent Among Older Populations," Census.gov, October 8, 2021, https://www.census.gov /library/stories/2021/04/love-and-loss-among-older-adults .html.